Computer Crime

Phreaks, Spies, and Salami Slicers

Karen Judson

—Issues in Focus—

ENSLOW PUBLISHERS, INC.

Bloy St. and Ramsey Ave.	P.O. Box 38
Box 777	Aldershot
Hillside, N.J. 07205	Hants GU12 6BP
U.S.A.	U.K.

Library of Congress Cataloging-in-Publication Data

Judson, Karen, 1941- .
    Computer crime: phreaks, spies, and salami slicers / Karen Judson.
       p. cm.—(Issues in focus)
    Includes bibliographical references and index.
    ISBN 0-89490-491-4
       1. Computer crimes—Juvenile literature. [1. Computer crimes.]
    I. Title. II.Series: Issues in focus (Hillside, N.J.)
    HV6773.J83 1994
    364.1'68—dc20   93-41198
                                            CIP
                                            AC

Printed in the United States of America

10 9 8 7 6 5 4 3 2 1

Illustration Credits:
Hayes Microcomputer Corp., pp. 26, 28; IBM Archives, pp. 16, 18, 21;
Karen Judson, pp. 49, 102; Mitsubishi Electric, from the Library of
Congress, p. 13; School of Engineer and Applied Science, University of
Pennsylvania, p. 15.

Cover Illustration:
©The Stock Market / Michael Newler, 1991

Contents

Acknowledgements

I would like to thank Joseph S. Valacich, Assistant Professor, Decision and Information Systems Department, Indiana University, Bloomington, Indiana; and Detmar W. Straub, Associate Professor of CIS, College of Business Administration, Georgia State University, Atlanta, Georgia, for their comments and assistance.

1

Arrested!

Robert Tappan Morris's friends described the tall, thin young man as a quiet, shy person. He was a good student, they said, especially in math and computer science, who spent most of his time outside the classroom fiddling with computers. On the surface he did not seem the type to plot a crime that would capture the attention of the entire nation.

On the night of November 2, 1988, however, Morris entered the computer room in Upson Hall on the campus of Cornell University in Ithaca, New York, for a purpose other than schoolwork. The twenty-three-year-old graduate student sat down at the keyboard of one of the machines, then nervously typed in a program that had taken him months to write. At that moment, Morris was to claim later, it didn't occur to him that he was committing an illegal act.

Cornell's computers were tied into the Internet/Arpanet communications networks, which connect some 85,200 computers at universities, government agencies, and businesses. The networks send information, ranging from unclassified military data to personal notes, from one computer to another, over ordinary telephone lines. On that fateful night in November, the network also innocently sent Morris's "worm"—a program that reproduces itself inside a computer and spreads to other machines, but, unlike a "virus," it does not destroy data.

Once inside a computer, Morris's invader worm attacked through three sets of commands: One set told the computer to copy the original program hundreds of times. A second searched out the names of all rightful users of the system and determined their passwords. The third told the computer to send copies of the original program to every other system it could reach.

Morris later said he created the program as an experiment, intending that it slowly and harmlessly copy itself across the networks. Instead, he made a programming mistake that caused the worm to reproduce much more quickly than he had planned. Like a fast-growing parasite, the program soon brought all normal functions of host computers to a halt by clogging them with unwanted electronic files. Estimates of the number of machines brought to a standstill as a result of the attack ranged from three thousand to sixty-two hundred.

Morris's worm did not destroy data stored in the infected computers, but it disrupted work—in some cases for as long as a week—and it seriously compromised confidence in the networks. The Computer Virus Industry Association estimated total damage in lost work, lost user hours, and manhours required to deworm infected systems at over $98 million.[1] Other estimates place the cost at a more modest $10 million.

"The kid simply put us out of action," summed up one federal government computer expert.[2] "The kid" was traced to his crime because he "signed" his work with his initials, and because he admitted to a friend what he had done. Ironically, one of the computer-security experts who helped trace the culprit was Bob Morris, Sr., a scientist at the National Computer Security Center in Maryland, and Robert's father. (Just a year before the worm incident, Robert, Sr., had asked his son to give a talk for U.S. National Security Agency officials, detailing how computer users can invade a system without getting caught.)

A few years earlier, Morris's act might have been seen as an infuriating prank that made system operators aware of security flaws. But by 1988, computer tampering laws had been in place for two years, and unauthorized entry into a computer system was against the law.

In July 1989, Robert Tappan Morris was charged under the 1986 Computer Fraud and Abuse Act—the federal law that makes it a crime for an unauthorized person to enter a computer system. He was tried in Syracuse, New York, in January 1990. Morris was found guilty by a jury, sentenced to three years probation and 400 hours of community service, and fined ten thousand dollars. He was also expelled from Cornell.

The Computer Access Issue

Robert Tappan Morris's act was especially newsworthy, not just for its scope, but because it focused attention on the vulnerability of linked computers and the consequences of computer crime—both to victims and perpetrators.

It also brought about a showdown between the two sides of the computer access issue.

On one side are civil libertarians and those who favor unrestricted access to information, such as the information industry, communications-service providers, and the curiosity-driven whiz kids called "hackers" (expert computer users). Prosecute computer criminals, this side says, but don't stifle the free exchange of information, and don't deny access to those whose motives are purely intellectual.

On the other side of the argument are privacy advocates, government agencies, law enforcement officials, and businesses who depend on the data stored in computers. From their point of view, anyone who breaks into a computer is an electronic Peeping Tom and a trespasser. Computers and the information they contain are private property, they say, and should not be invaded.

Since the Morris worm, the issue of computer access has raised many serious questions. How can those who control electronic data increase security without making it too difficult for legitimate users to access the computers? Can the government protect computer networks by means of laws against abuse, without destroying those networks? Or without violating civil rights?

How broad should the definition of crime be, as applied to computers? Should operators who steal computer time or services but do no damage be prosecuted as criminals? Is it time for hackers to rethink their free-wheeling behavior of the past?

Most important, as dependent as society has become on computers, can we guarantee the security for electronically stored information yet preserve personal rights and freedoms?

2

Computerizing Society

Computer "Fatal" to Hartford, Connecticut Voters![1]

Newspaper reports of computer foul-ups are not uncommon. But the September 30, 1992, issue of *USA Today* headlined what was probably the first-ever case of mass murder by a computer.

"In a modern-day twist to deadly plagues of yore, a 20th century computer has silently and painlessly 'killed' 5,500 Hartford, Conn., residents," read the article.

What happened? On Hartford's computerized list of registered voters, the city's name was placed in the wrong blank, pushing the last letter—the "d" in Hartford—into the next column. In that spot, "d" meant dead.

The registered voters list was used to select people for federal grand juries. Since Hartford names were listed as "dead," those individuals were, of course, all excluded from jury duty. The error was found when lawyers questioned why no one from the city was ever on the jury list for the U.S. District Court in the Hartford area.

The computer didn't actually kill anyone, of course, but this well-publicized error illustrates just how dependent upon computers our society has become. In fact, we use computers so extensively for keeping track of data that it's hard to remember what life was like without the machines.

The First Computers

Primitive peoples had no need for recording large numbers. They kept count by scratching in the dirt, or by tallying fingers and toes. But as civilization progressed, people needed to do more complex calculations to handle trade, agriculture, navigation, and the population. Since the human brain has a hard time remembering and handling large numbers, early inventors developed machines that could do the job.

In the early Middle Ages, for example, the Chinese and Japanese added, subtracted, multiplied, and divided numbers with an abacus, a device made up of rows of wooden rods and beads within a frame.

In 1642 Frenchman Blaise Pascal invented the first mechanical adding machine. He called his invention the Pascaline, and sold it to the public through ads that offered: "a small machine of my own invention, by means of which you . . . may perform all the operations of arithmetic, and may be relieved of the work which has often times fatigued your spirit."[2]

Englishman Charles Babbage began work on his Difference Engine in 1823. Powered by a steam engine and a system of weights, the machine could perform exponential functions and could figure square roots, cube roots, and interest rates. It printed out results and kept calculations in a crude form of storage. Although the Engine was never completed beyond the demonstration stage, its concept of machine-based computation provided a base for future inventors to build on.

American Herman Hollerith won the contract for the 1890 U.S. census count by showing government officials what his homemade counting machine could do. Called the world's first data processor, the machine used punched paper cards the size of dollar bills to count and sort the census data. To market his invention, Hollerith later founded the company that became the International Business Machines Corporation (IBM).

Developing the Electronic Brain

The invention of electricity was a turning point in the development of computers. By performing one basic function—switching electrical voltage on and off at lightning speed—electronic computers were able to process information at a much faster rate than any of the earlier computation machines.

The switches inside computers were and are the key to their performance. Located first in vacuum tubes, then in transistors, and today in microchips, the switches open and close when exposed to an electrical current. All electronic computers—from the first to modern-day—are run by programs (lists of instructions) that are made up of a complex series of *1s* and zeros, called a binary code. The bits, or characters in the binary code, determine whether a switch will open or close. When a low-voltage current is applied to a switch, it is read as a

Herman Hollerith's electrical tabulator was used to count the U.S. Census in 1890. This photograph, taken in 1908, shows an operator at the keyboard.

zero, and the switch is said to be closed. A high-voltage current represents a one, which opens the switch.

Before the invention of transistors, glass vacuum tubes regulated the flow of electricity inside computers. These tubes were controlled by dozens of switches that had to be set by hand. Cables were plugged into sockets one at a time to connect various parts of the system. Once entered in the computer, problems could take days or weeks to solve.

The largest and most powerful electronic vacuum tube computer of its day was the Electronic Numerical Integrator and Computer (ENIAC), built at the University of Pennsylvania in 1946. ENIAC was designed in response to the need to provide firing tables for new artillery in World War II. The mammoth machine weighed 30 tons and filled a 30-by-50-foot room. It cost $3,223,846 to build, and took 140 kilowatts of power and 18,000 vacuum tubes to run. ENIAC was more than a thousand times faster than any previous computer, but was so complicated to program and run that its use was severely restricted.[3]

Electronic computers were faster than their forerunners, but early versions like ENIAC were large and expensive, broke down a lot, and had to be kept in special temperature-and-humidity-controlled rooms. Information was entered on punched paper cards, or on paper tape with coded holes punched in at intervals, and the machines were cumbersome to operate.

The introduction of transistorized computers in 1958 marked the beginning of a new era in data processing. Transistors are microscopically small electronic devices that act as switches by allowing passage of an

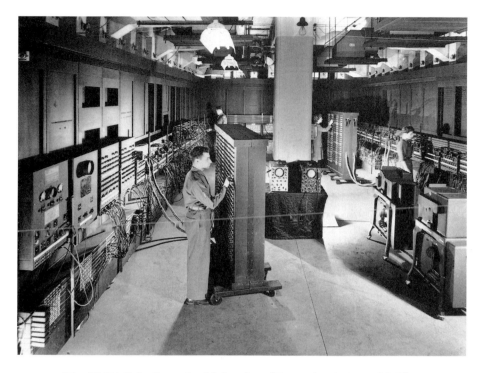

The ENIAC, built at the University of Pennsylvania in 1946. The machine occupied a room 30'x 50'. The controls are at the far left and a small part of the output device is seen at the right.

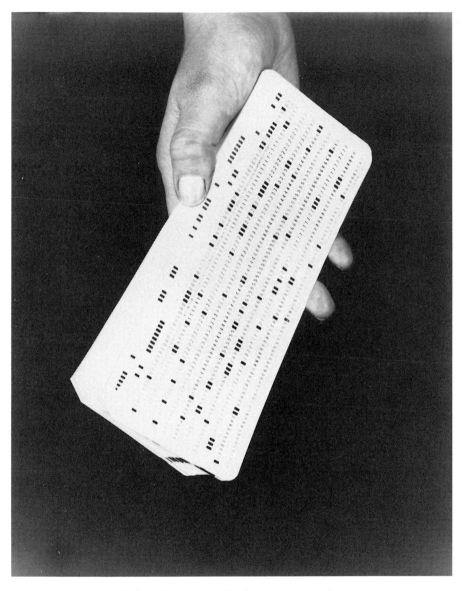

A punched card, used to feed information to early computers.

electrical current or blocking its flow. The new transistors were much smaller than vacuum tubes, used less power, and gave off less heat. Transistorized computers were five times faster than the older vacuum-tube models.[4]

Languages and Operating Systems

Programming computers became a little easier in the 1950s, when researchers developed simple computer languages called assembly languages. These special languages allowed programmers to use short letter combinations to relay instructions to the computer. The letter combinations stood for binary sequences the machine could understand. The first commercial computer, Remington Rand's 1951 UNIVAC, and the series of IBM computers that came out in 1953 used assembly languages written specifically for them.

Up to this point, however, computers had functioned without an operating system—a program that controls all of the machine's resources, from memory to printers and monitors. Computers with no operating system were extremely difficult to program and were slow in processing instructions, since thousands of commands were needed to accomplish a single task.

Then, in 1956 Bob Patrick, a programmer at General Motors, collaborated with Owen Mock, an engineer from North American Aviation, to develop a three-phase operating system for IBM computers that revolutionized computing. Using this system, called GM-NAA I/O, an IBM 704 computer could do twenty times more work, in a given time period, than the earlier 701 model.

As assembly languages and operating systems continued

The IBM 650 Computer, circa 1953. This series of computers used assembly languages written especially for them.

to evolve, each new development added to the speed, reliability, and user-friendliness of computers.

By 1966 IBM had developed an operating system for its System/360 computers that was a milestone in computer usability. Older, less complex operating systems met the needs of specific groups, such as scientists or businesses. But OS/360 provided for a wide range of applications that could be used by everyone from college students to NASA. IBM filled a thousand orders a month for its System/360 machines in 1966. At the end of that year there were more than 35,000 computers in use in the United States.[5]

Microprocessors Lead to Desktop Computers

When Intel introduced the world's first microprocessor, or microchip, in 1970, a new generation of computers was born. The 4004 microchip contained 2,250 transistors, imbedded in a tiny fleck of silicon (an abundant element found in rocks and sand). It could perform all the functions of a computer's central processing unit. Computers made with the new microchips were small enough to sit on a desktop, and were more reliable, faster, and cheaper than earlier machines.

By 1980, programs designed for use as operating systems, such as Microsoft's Disk Operating System (MS-DOS), made writing programs for and using computers easier than ever before. As a result, more persons learned to use computers, and in 1981 alone the use of personal computers increased threefold.

The number of computer users spiraled again with the 1983 release of the movie *War Games,* about a high-school student who nearly started a world war by using a home computer to gain entry into defense department computers.[6] By the end of the 1980s it was clear that computers were not only here to stay, but that they would continue to influence all aspects of society.

Today's Computers

The personal computers used by high-school students today are thirty to forty times faster than the 30-ton ENIAC built in 1946, and are sold at a tiny fraction of the cost. If cars had followed the same price versus performance development as computers, we could now buy a Rolls Royce for $2.75 that would get three million miles to the gallon, have enough power to move an ocean liner, and be fast enough to cross the continental United States in less than five minutes.[7]

The first electronic computers were all what are called mainframes, but today there are four general types of computers in use: supercomputers, mainframe computers, minicomputers, and personal computers.

Supercomputers are used extensively by researchers to solve complex problems or to map complicated data, such as the distances between stars, or the wind patterns in a storm. They average 10,000,000,000 (ten billion) operations per second.

Mainframe computers are used by big businesses and government agencies to perform large-scale tasks like counting the census or scanning income tax returns. They can perform over 100,000,000 (one hundred million) operations per second.

Minicomputers are purchased by businesses, to keep

The IBM Stretch 7030 looked like a machine from a science fiction movie.

personnel and payroll records, track inventory, and perform other business functions. They process over 1,000,000 (one million) operations per second.

Personal computers (PCs), or microcomputers, are most often bought for business use and are also used in homes and schools. Due to the thousands of programs now available for PCs, users can play games, write books, solve math problems, and even research term papers (with the help of a modem) on their personal computers. At 100,000 operations per second, these computers are surprisingly fast.

Here is a handy comparison of the power (expressed as performance time) of the different types of computers: An operation that takes 1 second to complete on a supercomputer takes 2 minutes on a mainframe, 2.75 hours on a minicomputer, and 33.6 hours on a PC or microcomputer.

Computer Basics

Regardless of size, the working parts of all computers are basically the same. The minimal amount of equipment needed to create a functional computer includes: the keyboard, the system unit, and the monitor or video display screen. *Hardware* refers to the physical equipment, both basic and optional, that makes up a computer system. *Software* is the term used for the instructions (programs) that make a computer perform its various functions.

The keyboard is patterned after the keys on a typewriter, and is used to type into the computer the commands and information needed to run a program.

Information may also be entered into the computer by use of a mouse (an attachment that lets the user choose from menus on the monitor screen), and, in computers with touch-screens, by touching with your finger choices displayed on the screen.

The system unit is the heart of the computer. It consists of the central processing unit (CPU), memory, disk drives, and various adapters and options. The CPU is the computer's brain. It runs programs, which are lists of instructions that tell the computer how to use incoming data.

The memory of the computer stores information to be processed by the CPU. Memory is measured in bytes. The meaning of the term "byte" is lost in history, but it typically equals eight bits, the basic unit of measurement in computing. A bit is a single binary digit—either a 1 or a zero—represented by low-voltage and high-voltage current applied to switches (transistors) inside the microchips. Since the measurement is not exact, a kilobyte (K) actually equals about 1,024 bytes, and a megabyte (Mb) equals approximately 1,048,576 bytes.

A computer has two kinds of memory. Random-access memory (RAM) is used to store and retrieve all types of information. Data stored in RAM is lost when the computer is turned off, unless the user first stores the information to disk before turning off the machine. For example, you type a letter using a word processing program. The letter is temporarily stored in RAM while you are writing it, but it will be lost when you turn off the computer unless you first give the command to store it to disk.

The second type of memory in a computer is called

ROM, for read-only memory. ROM permanently stores information that the computer needs to operate when in use. (This information is usually installed by the computer manufacturer and cannot be changed; it can only be read.) ROM, for example, stores the first program to run when the computer is turned on. This program is called the bootstrap loader. The bootstrap loader retrieves the operating system (for example, MS-DOS). The operating system is like a master switchboard that allows all other programs, such as word processing or accounting, to be run. Unlike RAM, the data in ROM is not lost when the computer is turned off.

The disk drive reads and writes information to or from a diskette. Disk drives are housed in the system unit, and may be floppy or fixed. A fixed or hard disk is a high-speed, large-capacity disk drive. The hard disk cannot be removed from the disk drive. A fixed disk can hold much more information than the floppy, or removable, diskette.

The monitor is the televisionlike screen that displays information typed into the computer, and lets the user interact with the machine. Some monitors show images only in black and white, while others are capable of a multicolor display.

Most computers have an attached printer that prints information out on paper. The three main types of printers are daisy-wheel or letter-quality, dot matrix, and laser printers. Daisy-wheel printers produce type by rotating and striking letters across an inked ribbon cartridge, much like a typewriter. In dot matrix printers, pins controlled by springs and magnets strike an inked ribbon to form letters or graphic images made up of tiny inked dots. Laser printers generate and use radio frequency energy to produce a concentrated beam of light (laser beam). The laser beam creates an image made up of dots on a photosensitive drum. A powder, called toner, is applied to the drum, and sticks to the dots, forming letters and graphics. The image is then heat-set on the paper.

The modem, a device for communicating with other computers across telephone lines, is an equipment option. Modems may be installed inside the system unit as special circuit cards (internal modems), or they may be connected to the computer externally (external modems). The telephone line is connected to the modem, which is, in turn, connected to the computer.

The modem (short for modulator-demodulator) translates the computer's digital pulses (a series of *1*s and zeros) to analog (continuous) sound waves, which can be transmitted over telephone lines much like the human voice. This is called modulation. The modem connected to the computer at the receiving end then translates the analog waves back to digital form (demodulation), so the computer can read the message. A special communications program is needed to run a modem. Increasingly, manufacturers are including built-in modems as standard equipment in personal computers.

Inside an Operating System

The operating system is the program that controls the computer. When the computer system is turned on, part of the operating system is always contained in the machine's main memory, and part of it is contained on

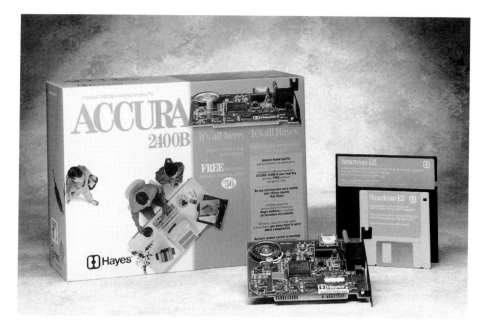

An internal modem, with the software requried to operate it. When connected to the telephone line and a computer, it allows the user to communicate with other computers.

the system disk, to be read into the memory only as necessary. Microsoft's Disk Operating System (MS-DOS) is a commonly used advanced program that allows the computer to keep track of files, run and link programs, and access attached devices, such as printers and disk drives.

Networks Come On-Line

Modems made possible the establishment of networks, linking computers in distant locations. Networks allowed computer users around the globe to exchange information simply by dialing a telephone number.

Wide Area Networks (WANs), which require the use of satellites and cables designed to handle data transmission, allow large numbers of computers to communicate. The world's first wide area network, named the Arpanet for its developer (the Pentagon's Advanced Research Projects Agency) began operating in 1969. It linked together computers used by researchers for the U.S. Department of Defense. The Arpanet eventually became part of a complex of networks called the Internet, which was developed in the mid-1980s. The Internet now links almost 1.5 million computers worldwide.[8]

Local Area Networks (LANs) tie computers together within smaller areas, such as within a single building or company. LANs join computers via copper wire, coaxial cables, telephone lines, or through thin fiber-optic lines that transmit signals as rapid pulses of light. Fiber-optic cables are made up of twenty-four hair-thin glass strands that can carry one hundred times more information than copper telephone lines.[9]

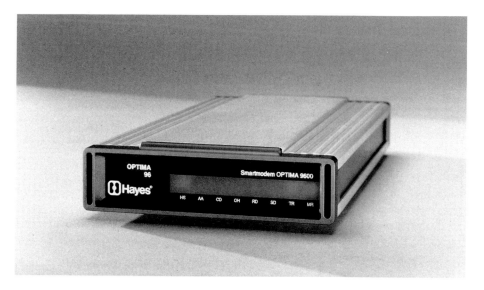

An external modem, which functions the same as an internal modem, but is connected outside the computer.

In the 1970s, Bell Telephone Labs developed technology that allows low-cost communication in data, voice, video, and graphic media over existing telephone lines. The 1984 breakup of American Telephone & Telegraph (AT&T) shelved work on a system called Integrated Services Digital Network (ISDN), but backers are hopeful that the service will soon be available nationwide. Since the network can relay information in digital form, modems would no longer be necessary for sending data between computers. Information that now takes several minutes to send could be zipped to the receiver in seconds.[10]

In 1993, the U.S. Congress began hearing pro and con arguments for a national information highway, using fiber-optic networks. Linkups would be available to every computer user, so students anywhere could use desktop computers to tap into libraries, doctors in distant cities could use video teleconferencing to treat a patient, and more workers could toil at home.[11]

Wireless communication is now available that will make possible telephone and computer communication, without the use of lines and cables.

Computer Crime: The Early Days

In *Techno-Crimes, The Computerization of Crime and Terrorism,* August Bequai writes that the first reported case of computer crime dates back to 1958, and the first federal prosecution to 1966.[12]

Donn B. Parker, author of *Crime By Computer* and *Fighting Computer Crime,* reported 374 cases of "computer abuse" from 1954 to 1976. (In four of these cases, the computer was actually shot by frustrated users. Two of the four "wounded" machines were a total loss; the remaining two were dented by bullets but bravely continued to run.)[13]

Well-known early cases include:

1954: The first documented case of "phone phreaks" breaking into the Bell Telephone System occurs. They used technical details of frequencies published by the company.

1964: Robert F. Hancock tried to sell $5 million worth of stolen software to the Texaco Company.

1967: A hacker gained access to confidential military information in the computers of the Strategic Air Command Headquarters in Omaha, Nebraska.

1969: A computer tape belonging to the Canadian International Development Agency was sent to a phony company.

1970: Two employees of a Swedish company sold copies of their firm's computer data to competitors.

1971: Angry employees of the Honeywell Corporation in Minneapolis, Minnesota, disabled the Metropolitan Life computer network for over a month.

Computer Crime on the Rise in the 1970s and 1980s

On-line networks, developed through the 1970s and 1980s, exposed computers to outside attack by those hackers who had a misguided sense of playfulness and who used their skills for personal gain, or to get even for perceived wrongs. By this time, more students were learning the secrets of computing. And more individuals had jobs in computer operations as systems administrators and analysts, programmers, data entry clerks, and repairpersons. This meant that more and more people knew computer systems, thus increasing the chances the machines would be misused in illegal or unethical ways.

As we might expect from increased knowledge and use of computers, losses from computer crime have also increased. According to the National Center for Computer Crime Data, American businesses lose over $550 million every year to computer-related crime in lost productivity and related costs. The figure reaches $1 billion if the salaries of the personnel who spend time fighting computer crime are included. This figure does not include the amount of money lost by consumers in schemes involving wire and the computer fraud.[14]

A 1984 survey of three hundred top U.S. corporations by the American Bar Association (ABA) reported that annual losses arising from computer crime ranged from $2 million to $10 million per company. In "Assessing Security," a 1990 article for *LAN Magazine*, Peter Stephenson states that government agencies have estimated it can cost a business as much as $2,000 per megabyte to replace data lost to intrusion or accident.[15]

The Computer Emergency Response Team (CERT) at the Software Engineering Institute, Carnegie Mellon University, Pittsburgh, Pennsylvania, was created after the Morris worm incident to work with the Internet community in handling and preventing computer emergencies. CERT reports that the number of computer security threats to the Internet increased from 132 in 1989 to 252 in 1990. Hackers broke into

Internet 773 times in 1992, a 90 percent increase over the year before. CERT gets an average of 1,100 electronic mail messages daily from callers at computer sites on the Internet, either requesting help after a break-in, or asking for security tips to prevent a break-in.[16]

The exact cost of computer crime is hard to pinpoint, though. Because many businesses and agencies don't want the public to know that security has been breached, they do not report incidents. Experts estimate that only twenty to fifty percent of computer crimes are reported, because a successful fraud, if broadcast, can be a public relations disaster.

Clearly, criminal acts in *cyberspace,* a term for computer networks that was coined in 1982 by science-fiction writer William Gibson, have increased as computers have multiplied. As society has become increasingly dependent on computers, those skilled in their use have come up with new ways to misuse them.

"Cyberspace, in its present condition, has a lot in common with the 19th Century West," writes John Perry Barlow, songwriter for the Grateful Dead, co-founder of the Electronic Frontier Foundation, and computer wizard, in "Crime & Puzzlement: Desperados of the DataSphere." "It is vast, unmapped, culturally and legally ambiguous, verbally terse (unless you happen to be a court stenographer), hard to get around in, and up for grabs. Large institutions already claim to own the place, but most of the actual natives are solitary and independent, sometimes to the point of sociopathy. It is, of course, a perfect breeding ground for both outlaws and new ideas about liberty."[17]

Hacking U.S.A.

"Although it may not seem like it, I am pretty much a normal American teenager. I don't drink, smoke, or take drugs. I don't steal, assault people, or vandalize property. The only way I am really different from most people is in my fascination with the ways and means of learning about computers that don't belong to me."

The above quote is from *Out of the Inner Circle: A Hacker's Guide to Computer Security* by Bill Landreth, known on-line as "The Cracker." Landreth started hacking when he was fourteen years old, and joined the invitation-only Inner Circle hackers' group at sixteen. In 1983, when he was seventeen, he was convicted of computer fraud for tapping into the GTE Telemail computer network based in Virginia. He served three years probation.[1]

What Is A Hacker?

The term *hacker* was first used in the 1960s to describe college students at the Massachusetts Institute of

Technology (MIT) who couldn't get enough of computers. Desktop computers were not yet in use, and the students vied for time on the few mainframes available, writing their own programs for machines that were hidden away in the university's computer lab.

Hacker was a label of pride for those early programmers, who preferred punching a keyboard to eating, sleeping, bathing, studying, or socializing with nonhackers. They loved to probe a system—the bigger the better—to find out how it worked, and to learn how to make it give up its secrets. These hackers believed computer time, know-how, and software should be free and freely shared, and they resented those who would protect ownership. At the same time, early hackers had strict unwritten rules against erasing or damaging others' files, changing data, or using a system for personal gain.

In *The Hacker's Dictionary: A Guide to the World of Computer Wizards,* Guy Steele and his co-authors list seven accepted definitions of the word *hacker*:

1. Someone who enjoys learning every detail about computers as opposed to most users of computers, who only learn what is necessary to perform certain functions.

2. One who loves programming, rather than just theorizing about programming.

3. A person who appreciates "hack value." (A hack is a clever computer deed. The hack has value when others admire its daring and originality.)

4. One who is good at programming quickly.

5. An expert on a certain program.

6. A computer expert of any kind.

7. A malicious or curious intruder who tries to discover information by breaking into a computer system.[2]

Unfortunately, *hacker* has gradually evolved from a label denoting competence and knowledge to a term meaning someone who breaks into computers.

Who Are the Hackers?

The Federal Bureau of Investigation (FBI) has compiled a profile of the typical computer intruder. Most are between eighteen and thirty-five years of age, says Harold Hendershot, supervisory special agent in computer fraud and abuse for the FBI. They are bright, highly motivated, adventuresome, creative, and they love a challenge. They are the first workers on the job in the morning, and the last to leave at night, and they are usually among the most trusted employees. Most are male. However, more females are hacking, as larger numbers of women enter the workplace and become more technologically oriented.[3]

In a five-year study completed in 1988, Joan McCord, professor of criminal justice at Temple University in Philadelphia, Pennsylvania, found that female college students were more likely to see computer crime as wrong than were male students. Further, she says, those "students least likely to condemn using computers as tools for crime presented profiles similar to those one would expect from prior research about street criminals. Compared with their classmates, they were more aggressive and less interested in the welfare of others. They were unlikely to be interested in school or to have strong academic commitments."[4]

Computer criminals have tended to be amateurs,

Hendershot adds, "until recently. Now we are seeing a trend where hackers are motivated by profit."

"We are seeing a shift," confirms Scott Charney, chief of computer crime for the U.S. Justice Department. Hackers arrested for the first time are older than in the past—in their twenties and thirties—and motives are changing. "The pure hacker ethic—'We want to explore the system; we don't want to do any damage; we don't want to steal anything'—may still exist," he says. "But more and more we are seeing cases where that ethic does not exist, and there is an ulterior motive, such as profit.

"For example," continues Charney, "we indicted these hackers in New York—the Masters of Deception. We did electronic surveillance, and these hackers were accessing credit card companies. By the end of the investigation, they were selling the information. If they were ever pure hackers, they reached a point where they saw a profit potential, and they started selling the stuff. . . . As more people get their hands on computers, the fear is that those people who don't want to use them properly will not use them properly."[5]

Eugene Spafford, a computer science professor and computer security expert at Purdue University, in West Lafayette, Indiana, disputes the common assumption that all computer intruders are exceptionally intelligent. "The popular conception people have is that these guys who break in [to computer systems] are incredibly talented in some way. Basically, the reason they get in is that they are persistent, and they communicate well.

"Really, they aren't very innovative," Spafford adds.

"They just have a list of things to try to exploit some common flaws in systems. Basically, the people who administer the systems either made a mistake, or are simply not that concerned with high security, because of what they have on the system. [Intruders] pick up recipes on bulletin boards for breaking into systems, and they follow them step-by-step, including some steps that are totally unnecessary. But they don't understand that, because they don't know how the system works; sometimes they get in."[6]

Why Do Hackers Hack?

Hackers who break into computer systems nearly always argue, when caught, that they were simply curious; they wanted to learn more. "That sounds very heroic," says Marty Flynn, computer and network security specialist for AT&T, "but it's against the law. . . . You wouldn't go into somebody's house without permission, or take things, and a computer is somebody's property. Somebody owns not only the physical computer, but also the information on it . . .[7]

Chris Goggans, once a member of the hacker Legion of Doom club, who was known on-line as "Erik Bloodaxe," admits that some hackers commit illegal acts, but argues in the June 8, 1992 issue of *Computerworld*: ". . . they are still hardly criminal in nature. The intention of most of these individuals is not to destroy or exploit systems but to learn in minute detail how they are used and what they are used for. The quest is purely intellectual, but the drive to learn is so overwhelming that any obstacle blocking its course will be circumvented.

Unfortunately, the obstacles are usually state and federal laws on unauthorized computer access . . ."[8]

An interest in computing is most often healthy and rewarding. But experts claim that some hackers may be drawn to computers for the anonymity they allow. The nameless, faceless environment may encourage those personality types most likely to commit malicious or criminal acts if given the opportunity to remain unknown. "We can presume that there will always be a percentage of the population that is criminal in nature," says Charney. "You give these people computers—something like thirty percent of all American homes have computers—and you will have more computer criminals than you had before."

When Is Hacking a Crime?

In *Computer Ethics*, Tom Forester and Perry Morrison define computer crime as "a criminal act that has been committed using a computer as the principal tool."[9] Donn B. Parker, consultant to SRI International of Menlo Park, California, and author of *Crime by Computer*, defines computer abuse as "computer-related" and/or "computer-assisted" criminal activity.[10]

Most experts agree that illegal computer activities fall into three broad categories:

- Unauthorized access (entry) gained to satisfy a personal motive like curiosity, pride, or a sense of adventure.
- Unauthorized access to tamper with or to destroy information or operations, including initiating the spread of viruses.

- Unauthorized access to steal data or computer services or to perform acts for criminal purposes, such as credit card theft.

Computer Crime Legislation

Arizona was the first state to pass a law against computer crime, in 1979. To date, basic computer crime laws have been passed in forty-nine states. Vermont is the only state without such a law.

In 1980 the U.S. Copyright Act was amended to include software. Patent laws also protect some software and hardware, and contract laws may protect trade secrets.

Those computer crimes not covered by existing state and federal laws are covered by the 1986 Computer Fraud and Abuse Act. The law covers computer espionage, theft of financial information, trespass into U.S. government computers, trespass into "federal-interest computers" with intent to defraud, and trespass into a federal-interest computer to alter or destroy information.

The FBI and the U.S. Secret Service (USSS) have joint jurisdiction to enforce this law. The FBI handles violations involving espionage, terrorism, organized crime, and threats to national security. The Secret Service investigates crimes involving computers used by the Treasury Department, and those involving computers that contain information protected by the Financial Privacy Act, such as credit card information, credit-reporting information, and data maintained on bank loan applications.

Violation of this law is a felony (a crime punishable

by death or at least one year in prison), and convicted offenders face a maximum sentence of five years in prison and a $250,000 fine.[11]

The Electronic Communications Privacy Act of 1986 makes it a crime to break into any electronic communications service, including telephone services. The Computer Security Act of 1987 requires that security plans be put into place for "sensitive" civilian computer systems. The act assigned to the National Institute of Standards and Technology (NIST) the responsibility for advising and assisting federal agencies concerning computer security.[12]

Are Hackers a Threat?

Bruce Sterling, author of *The Hacker Crackdown,* questions the degree of threat posed by young curiosity-driven hackers, as opposed to insiders—those employees in computer operations who have the opportunity to commit electronic crimes. He estimates that as few as one hundred hackers are "skilled enough to penetrate sophisticated systems and truly to worry corporate security and law enforcement." However, he, too, warns that "electronic fraud, especially telecommunication crime, is growing by leaps and bounds."[13]

Richard Baker, author of *The Security Handbook* agrees that in today's world, the most troublesome threats to computer security include:

- Employees who commit computer-related fraud, while working within the affected companies themselves.
- Acts of vengeance by former employees with grievances.

40

- Industrial espionage and the loss of trade secrets.
- Use and misuse of electronic fund transfers.
- Computer errors and the corruption of data.
- The computerized invasion of personal privacy.[14]

In an article for *Sloan Management Review*, Detmar Straub, Jr., associate professor of computer information systems at Georgia State University in Atlanta, and Jeffrey Hoffer, professor of operations and systems management at Indiana University in Bloomington, report that the employees who most often abuse systems are application programmers. "They are followed by three categories of frequent system users (clerical personnel, system users, and managers) that together account for two out of five abuses in business organizations," say the authors.

The study also found: "The overwhelming majority of offenders were employees or ex-employees, which reinforces the notion that those with direct system contact are more likely to commit abuses. Hackers are a threat, but insiders are a more pressing threat.

"Offenders appear to have been motivated almost equally by desire for personal gain, ignorance of proper professional conduct, and misguided playfulness; a smaller group was motivated by maliciousness."[15]

The word *hacker* has come to mean "one who breaks into computer systems," an activity that is now against the law. But the threat to computer security from hackers is not as great as most people believe. Company and organizational insiders are far more dangerous.

4

Stealing Money

"You're not as smart as you think you are," U.S. District Court Judge Harry Leinenweber told convicted embezzler Armand Moore in September 1989, as he sentenced Moore to ten years, five months in prison. Moore and four accomplices were convicted in June 1989 of plotting to transfer money electronically from accounts at the First National Bank of Chicago to a bank in Austria. The swindlers, with the help of a bank employee, illegally transferred a total of $69 million from the accounts of Merrill Lynch investment company, Brown-Forman Corporation, and United Airlines. They confessed to planning to steal $236 million in all. Assistant U.S. Attorney Jeff Stone asked for the maximum sentence for Moore, calling the scam "the most massive and almost successful computer crime I'm aware of in the history of the United States."

Judge Leinenweber called the crime "stupid," because the five transferred the money over a weekend, then were quickly discovered when they could not immediately withdraw the stolen funds. The day after the transferral, Moore shopped for a $50,000 Jaguar. He was also making plans to buy three homes. "He was trying to spend the money before he got it," the prosecuting attorney told the jury. All five men received prison sentences.[1]

When the motive for a computer crime is profit, the stakes can be high. A 1990 report, "Computers at Risk," issued by the National Research Council, warned that "the modern thief can steal more with a computer than with a gun." In *Computer Security Handbook*, Richard H. Baker notes that the average computer crime nets the crook $650,000—more than seventy-two times the amount of an average bank robbery.

Who Are Today's Techno-Bandits?

Those who use computers to steal money generally fall into one of three groups, listed here in the order of the threat they pose:

1. Current or former computer operations employees.

2. Career criminals who use computers to ply their trade.

3. The hacker, as defined in Chapter 3.

Outsiders who break into systems are sometimes a threat, but employees or ex-employees are usually in a better position to steal. Because we rely more and more on computers, we also depend more on those who make them and run them. (The U.S. Bureau of Labor Statistics projects that the fastest growing employment opportunities from 1986 to 2000 will be in computer and data-processing services.) Since money is a common motive for those who use their computing know-how to break the law, losses from computer theft are expected to grow as the number of computer employees rises.

Employees Work Overtime

In 1980, two enterprising ticket agents for Trans World Airlines (TWA) discovered how to make their employer's computer work for them. The scam went like this: When a passenger used cash to pay for a one-way ticket, Vince Giovengo sent in the credit charge form, which he should have discarded. He kept the receipt that should have been given to the passenger for paying cash. Samuel Paladino, who helped board passengers, kept the part of the traveler's ticket that should have been returned to the customer. The two agents used computers to reassemble the ticket from the pieces they had. They then marked the ticket void, and kept the cash the traveler had paid. The swindle was finally discovered by another employee who questioned the large numbers of voided tickets.

Giovengo and Paladino were tried in Pennsylvania and convicted of federal wire fraud for using their workplace computer to steal from the company.[2]

Another computer heist, one of the largest ever, involved several highly placed employees of the Volkswagen car company of West Germany. In 1987 the company discovered that these "loyal" workers had managed to steal $260 million by programming computers to disguise the company's foreign currency transactions.[3]

Career Criminals

When career criminals discover computers, they can often increase their take in a big way. In 1990, nearly one hundred counterfeit checks turned up in Tuscaloosa, Alabama. The checks, written for amounts that totaled tens of thousands of dollars, were traced to a high-tech operation in a private home. Police found a document scanner, a laser printer, a computer, and a disk filled with checks, drivers' licenses, and department store IDs. "The guy could copy anything he wanted," a Jackson, Mississippi police detective told *Time* magazine.[4]

Computer Theft Victims

Banks and brokerage houses are major targets when stealing money is the objective, because of their increased reliance on electronic funds transfer (EFT). Using EFT, American financial institutions and federal and state governments pass back and forth over the telephone lines nearly one trillion dollars in funds and assets every day. The money transferred from bank to bank, or from payers' accounts to payees' accounts, is moved by utilizing telephone messages between computers. Following coded instructions, a computer in the sending location subtracts the amount to be transferred from the appropriate account, and a computer in the receiving location adds the transferred amount to the designated account.

In the old days, B.[efore] C.[omputers], transferring money between banks usually involved armored cars and armed security guards. Today, computer operators simply type in the appropriate instructions and funds are zipped across telephone lines from bank A to bank B.

In like manner, today's employees can sometimes choose to have their paychecks deposited directly into a bank account, instead of physically taking a printed check to the bank, standing in line, and depositing it. Similarly, many companies who bill consumers monthly, such as gas and electric utilities, offer the option of having the monthly service charges automatically deducted from the customer's bank account. No bill is mailed, and no check is written—the transaction takes place entirely between computers, using the telephone line.

But, at either end of these financial transactions, if the coded computer instructions are accidentally garbled—through human error or telephone equipment breakdown—or if they are deliberately changed, the transaction can go haywire. The wrong amount or no amount may be sent. The wrong account may be shorted, or the wrong one credited, as in the following case.

When a Los Angeles accountant was accused of stealing nearly $1 million from the United California Bank, he pled not guilty because of a computer mistake. His defense was that due to a keyboard typing error his account had been mistakenly credited with a deposit of $927,288. A jury found him not guilty.[5]

Automatic teller machines (ATMs) are also popular targets for thieves. According to the National Center for Computer Crime Data, in 1988 banks lost $13 million from unauthorized use of ATM cards, as well as $21 million from customer fraud and $3 million from other sources.[6]

The handy ATMs, located in bank lobbies and drive-up lanes, and in many restaurants, stores, and shopping malls, allow account holders to withdraw or deposit money without going to the bank and standing in line at a teller's window. Those bank account-holders who want them are issued coded plastic cards for use in the machines. After inserting the card, users type in a personal identification number (PIN), then indicate which transaction they want.

There have been cases where entire ATMs machines were carted off and pilfered, but most often, stolen or lost magnetic cards and PINs are used to raid ATM accounts. Sometimes thieves steal PINs simply by "piggy-backing" or "shoulder-surfing"—looking over the shoulders of legitimate customers while they are using the machines. They then enter the stolen numbers and withdraw money from victims' accounts.

The same method may be used to filch the fourteen-digit codes from users of telephone credit cards. Stolen codes may be sold on the street moments later, or used by the thief and his friends and family to make long-distance telephone calls at the victim's expense. An enterprising con artist can hang out at a bank of pay phones, eavesdrop for numbers, then feed them by beeper to an accomplice waiting at a different phone bank. The thief sells calls to any location in the world (which are billed to the stolen PIN) for $10 to $20 a pop. A cheater with a beeper and fast fingers can easily make $1,500 a day.[7]

Thieves who know the ins and outs of ATMs can also score big, like the thirty-five-year-old former ATM repairman caught in 1987 after stealing $86,000 from New York City's automatic teller machines. He shoulder-surfed for PINs and picked up receipts ATM customers had left. He was finally arrested after making a mistake in encoding a phony card. The ex-repairman called himself a "white-collar criminal," and he said he had hoped to be hired as a security expert by one of the banks he robbed.[8]

In another case, an installer of automated teller machines rigged a cash machine at a fast-food restaurant to allow him to collect the account numbers of all the machine's users before the numbers reached the bank. He had made 4,000 cardboard cards and was waiting for a long weekend to empty the machine when he was caught.[9]

One of the biggest ATM heists on record took place in the spring of 1993, when crooks pulled off what law enforcement authorities called "one of the most technologically sophisticated U.S. bank-fraud schemes ever." The thieves stole hundreds of thousands of dollars from ten Connecticut banks by placing a fake ATM in a Manchester, Connecticut, shopping mall. They rigged the machine to record users' account numbers and PINs then used the data to produce counterfeit cards. At first the thieves' machine dispensed money to customers on demand, but later transactions were rejected and cards were returned—after the confidential data had been secretly recorded.[10]

Insurance companies as well as banks are often the victims of computer theft. In one of the country's largest insurance scams, a company called the Equity Funding Corporation issued 64,000 fake insurance policies for resale to other insurers. The president of the company and several of his employees used a computer to make the false policies look like the company's legitimate

Personal Identification Numbers can be stolen by "shoulder surfing"—looking over the shoulder of a customer using an automatic teller machine.

policies. The group hid the fraud inside secret computer files for ten years, but they were finally exposed when the company failed.[11]

In another insurance con, a claims agent with a Florida company used her computer to steal more than $200,000 in a phony claims fraud. She was arrested and prosecuted under Florida's 1978 computer crime law.[12]

Computer skills have also benefited the credit-card encoding rings that have multiplied in the 1990s. In 1992 in the Los Angeles, California, area alone, police reported the existence of fifteen such rings. In August of that same year, Los Angeles investigators arrested a nineteen-year-old college student for credit-card fraud. In his apartment, they found a computer and an encoding device used to change the magnetic coding on credit cards.

The student had apparently lifted customer's credit-card numbers at the shoe store where he worked, then put the stolen credit-card numbers onto the magnetic strips of cards in his possession. He used some of the altered cards for personal purchases but sold others for up to $400 each.

Police said the suspect bought the encoder at a local computer store and used a modem to hook it up to his home computer. The encoders are sold to hospitals, schools, and businesses for legal uses, such as encoding identification cards.

Another California coding ring allegedly purchased valid credit-card numbers from a telephone-mail-order clerk at a store in New Jersey, then used the stolen numbers to get cash advances from banks in several states.

Visa International reported that losses from encoding

fraud jumped from zero in 1989 to $39 million in 1991. MasterCard said they had not isolated losses from encoding fraud, but they expected them to be comparable to Visa's.[13]

After the California arrests, a police detective told a reporter for the *Los Angeles Times*: "There are some detectives who believe that re-encoding credit cards is going to be the savings and loan debacle of the '90s."[14]

Data Diddling, Salami Slicing, and Blackmail

Honest mistakes sometimes happen, but in many criminal cases involving EFT and other electronic communications, the coded messages that make the computer transaction possible have been deliberately changed by someone who knows the system.

The act of changing data going into a computer, or during output from a computer, is called "data diddling." Donn B. Parker reports in *Fighting Computer Crime* that a New Jersey bank suffered a $128,000 loss when the manager of computer operations made changes in account balances to correct some errors. Since the regular error correction program was not working properly, it was easy for the operations manager to make changes. He transferred money from several accounts to the accounts of three of his friends.[15]

"Salami slicing" is a form of data diddling that occurs when an employee steals small amounts from a large number of sources through the electronic changing of data (like slicing thin pieces from a roll of salami). For example, in a bank, the interest paid to savings accounts may routinely be rounded to the nearest cent.

A dishonest computer programmer may change the round-down program slightly, so that all the remainders (fractions of a cent left after sums are rounded) go into an account that he has established for himself. The sums are small, but when taken from thousands of accounts over a period of time, they can add up to a large amount. And the theft is hard to detect because the books balance.

Several variations of salami slicing have been used by techno-bandits. A timekeeping clerk was arrested after she was discovered adding overtime to timecards she recorded; the extra payment was then diverted to her own account. A store's inventory was reduced by several small items each month; these were stolen by a dishonest employee who then later sold them for cash.

Sometimes greedy computer users use extortion to force a company to pay ransom. They plant destructive programs, then threaten to set them off if money is not paid, or they hold stolen programs or files hostage until the company pays up.

One of the oldest forms of criminal behavior, stealing money is here to stay. Today's digital desperados are usually classified as "white-collar criminals"—office workers who perform a minimum of physical labor. But they have also been called simply the most recent in a long line of historic crooks, from roadside robbers, to stagecoach bandits, to safe-crackers with high explosives.

Money is stolen on-line by thieves using computers, but the information stored in computers, and the actual on-line time used, also have cash value. In fact, computer data bases are especially tempting to burglars, because they can contain more treasures than a bank vault, and it isn't necessary to crack a safe to get at them.

5

Information Profiteers

John Draper, a.k.a. "Cap'n Crunch," earned his alias when he discovered that the whistle that came in Cap'n Crunch cereal was a perfect match for the 2600-hertz tone used by the telephone company's switching system. He found that the whistle's matching tone could be used to trick the system into granting free access to long-distance lines.

Draper got better and better at using the whistle, and was said to be the first "phone phreak" (a hacker who specializes in cracking telephone systems) who could bounce a call around the world, then back to himself. After he was featured in an article about hackers and phreaks in a 1971 issue of *Esquire*, Draper's telephone was tapped by the FBI. In 1972 he was caught while making an illegal call to Australia. He pled guilty to wire fraud, and was fined $1,000 and sentenced to five years probation.

Draper reportedly liked telling others about his

phreaking accomplishments as much as he liked making free long-distance calls. Shortly after his first probation ended, he was talked into making an illegal call by a friend; he was arrested again. He came up for sentencing before the same judge who had presided over his first case. "I told you that you would not be treated leniently again . . . , " the judge told Draper. "Your conduct is hard to reconcile with your intelligence. . . . I view this more seriously than other people."[1]

Cap'n Crunch served four months in prison after his second conviction, followed by another five years probation. After his release he held several jobs in computer operations, but again, could not stay away from phreaking. He wrote an automatic dialing program that took some of the manual labor out of his efforts. When he put it into use, he was caught and arrested again. He pled guilty to wire fraud and was sentenced to another year in jail.

At last report, though, John Draper was doing well as a computer professional and had finally shed the Cap'n Crunch persona.[2]

Phone Phreaks

The first hackers, even before the computer buffs at MIT, were phone phreaks. In fact breaking into telephone systems goes back almost as far as Alexander Graham Bell's invention of the telephone in 1876. Bruce Sterling claims in *The Hacker Crackdown* that the first teenage males were "flung off" the new telephone system by enraged authorities as early as 1878.[3]

As soon as long-distance calling began, phone

phreaks figured out how to use the service without paying for it. Before computers with modems, phone phreaks pioneered the "blue box"—a gadget that mimicked the phone switching system's high-pitched whistle, a 2600-hertz tone that signaled the equipment to release circuits. By holding the blue box up to a telephone receiver, users could call any long-distance number without a toll charge.

There are two versions of the story about the origin of the name *blue box*. One says that the first box confiscated by authorities was blue, giving the box its name.[4] The second says that phone phreaks discovered the telephone company's Multi-Frequency Signaling System in the *Bell System Technical Journal*, put out by Bell Labs for its network engineers. The journal had a blue cover and within the industry was called the "Blue Book," so naturally the phreaks called their electronic gadget the "blue box."[5]

Throughout the 1960s and into the 1970s, selling blue boxes was a source of spending money for many electronically savvy college students. (Steven Jobs and Steve Wozniak, founders of Apple Computer, sold homemade blue boxes in their undergraduate days—absolutely guaranteed—at the low price of $80 each.)[6]

Telephone companies have been popular victims of intruders for two reasons. First, they have always used the most powerful computers available, and this was a lure for any hacker itching to learn through practice. And second, "The Telephone Company" symbolized for many the greedy, uncaring bureaucracy, so they saw no harm in making what seemed a small dent in the enemy's bloated profits.

Phone phreaking was so popular that by the mid-1970s, American Telephone & Telegraph (AT&T) reported losing an estimated $30 million a year to telephone fraud.[7] And the problem grows yearly. In 1992, the Communication Fraud Control Association estimated losses from telecommunications fraud at $2.2 billion—up from $500 million in 1987 and $1.1 billion in 1991.[8]

Wireless Phreaking

Breaking into telephone company computers has continued to the present. Today's cellular telephones are also vulnerable to phone phreaks. Cellular chips can be reprogrammed to present a stolen or fake caller ID to which the call will be billed. But making the changes isn't easy, and a bungled job ruins the phone.

In August 1992, Orange County, California, got the bill for the cellular phones inside call boxes along the county's freeways. These cellular phones are to be used for emergency calls. Normally, something like 12,000 calls a month are made from the system's 1,150 call boxes (about 10 per box). But the August bill showed that in that one month, 11,733 calls were made from just *one* of the call boxes. According to monitoring computers, someone had chatted for 25,875 minutes, around the globe, at Orange County's expense.

With the help of the two cellular telephone companies that provide and maintain the service, authorities determined that a hacker had reprogrammed a cellular phone, using the code and telephone number for one of the call boxes. Because there were too many calls for one person to have made, officials believed the stolen numbers had been sold to others.

The culprits were not caught, but Orange County employees fixed the system, so hackers could no longer gain entry.[9]

PBX Fraud

Hackers have also used corporate private branch-exchange (PBX) phone systems to divert charges for long-distance calls. PBXs have a feature that allows company employees to dial into the home office—usually on an 800 line—from outside. After punching in a personal identification number, they get a second dial tone and can then make calls as if they were at work. This allows the company to save the additional fees that telephone companies charge for making calling-card calls.

Once they learn a company's 800 number, hackers can dial that number, then use re-dial programs to crack PINs and dial back out. The company is then billed as the source of the call.

Stealing Credit Information

The Secret Service claims that U.S. telephone companies and credit-card companies combined lose over $1 billion a year through the illegal use of stolen passwords and access codes.[10]

Hackers who steal credit card numbers for re-sale or personal use are called "carders." Some hacker groups consider carding the mark of thugs, but others specialize in the crime. MasterCard estimated $57 million was lost to counterfeit card scams in 1991, but they could not say what portion was due to carders.[11]

Credit-reporting agencies have become frequent hacker victims. In July, 1992, five hackers, all under the age of twenty-two, were arrested for breaking into the computer systems of several companies, including Southwestern Bell, Pacific Bell, and TRW, a credit-reporting agency. The crimes reportedly cost Southwestern Bell $370,000. The five, members of a hackers' group called the Masters of Disaster or Masters of Deception (MOD), allegedly stole telephone and credit account information from the companies, then sold the information.[12]

TRW was also victimized by a juvenile hacker in April of 1990, when a twelve-year-old Michigan boy gained illegal access to the company's computers. He was accused of distributing charge-card numbers he found in TRW's files to computer bulletin boards, which allowed anyone who accessed the bulletin boards to use the numbers.

The boy was charged with computer and financial transaction fraud. His computer and disks were seized from his home, after authorities determined the youth was "deeply involved" in the theft. No one knew how many files had been tapped, who used the credit card numbers, or what was purchased with them. TRW officials noticed the improper entry to their system and contacted authorities. The Michigan Computer Crime Task Force, made up of state and federal authorities, said the boy broke through TRW security at a Detroit-area branch.[13]

Social Engineering and Dumpster Diving

The data used to crack telephone systems is not always acquired through clever hacking. Many phone phreaks, including Cap'n Crunch, got the technical information they needed from the telephone companies by simply calling and asking for it. They used facts they had already learned to convince the person on the other end of the telephone that they were informed employees and were thus entitled to the information they requested. The technique is called "social engineering."

For example, a young man in California posed as a magazine writer to gain entry to a telephone company, where helpful employees answered his questions about the parts distribution system. He then used his computer to order parts and have them delivered to spots where he could easily pick them up. Before he was caught, he had started his own telephone equipment supply business, and had sold over $1 million worth of stolen parts.

"Dumpster diving" or "trashing" is another way to get company documents, credit card and telephone charge card numbers, and other restricted information. A person simply sifts through wastebaskets when left alone in an office, or visits the victim's garbage dumpster after closing to sift through the day's trash.

Hacker Groups and Bulletin Boards

The information retrieved through electronic browsing, social engineering, and trashing may be sold by the thief for a fee, or may simply be collected by a proud hacker as evidence of a clever hack. But trophies are useless if there's no one to admire them, and hackers, by nature, love to share their cagey deeds. Therefore, stolen information is often shared with other hackers by posting it on electronic bulletin boards for anyone on-line to read or download.

A bulletin board system is a means of passing information. It consists of a computer, special software, and a modem for taking incoming calls. The first computer bulletin board for PCs was started in 1978, and there are now over 40,000 boards in the United States. Bulletin boards serve 10.5 million users, and that number is expected to double by the year 2000.[14]

A bulletin board system may be operated by a large fee-for-use information service, such as CompuServe or The Source, or it may be run by one person, sometimes from the system operator's (SysOp) bedroom or garage. A bulletin board service may be free. Some bulletin boards require the caller to identify himself or herself with a password before using the system, but for others one need only dial the number to connect. Some bulletin boards have rules that callers must follow or risk being booted from the system, for example, no swearing, no preaching overthrow of the government, and no posting of stolen files. Other bulletin boards have no rules at all.

Hacker groups spawn new bulletin boards, and vice-versa. Fed by the bulletin board forum, the list of hacker groups grows yearly. Here are a few hacker groups from a list of 131 compiled by the editors of *Phrack* in 1988: Anarchy Inc., Circle of Death, Digital Gang, The Elite Hackers, 414s, The Inner Circle, Legion of Doom, Master Hackers, Masters of Disaster (or Masters of

Deception), nuPromethius, and Phone Phreakers of America.

As a rite of passage into "elite" hacker status, some groups encourage members to learn company or government agency computer access codes. The codes are then posted on "underground" bulletin boards—those specializing in covert information.

Arresting the Culprits

Police across the country sometimes run their own bulletin boards, snaring unwary hackers who use the service to post stolen information or to brag about exploits.

Law enforcement agencies also use court-authorized wiretaps to monitor voice conversations and data transmissions of hackers under suspicion. Evidence used in the arrest of the five members of MOD (reported above under "Stealing Credit Information") was obtained partially by wiretapping. Agents charged that the men carried on a conversation in which they asked for instructions on how to add and remove delinquency reports from certain credit histories. The hackers were allegedly overheard plotting to "destroy people's lives . . . or make them look like a saint."[15]

Phone phreaking and stealing electronic data for profit are two illegal acts that often go hand-in-hand with hacking. In one recent case that was successfully prosecuted, a busy thirty-six-year-old hacker, known underground as "Kyrie," was sentenced to twenty-seven months in prison for her deeds. Prosecutors charged that she had acquired 481 security codes, including PBX access codes, credit-card numbers for four major credit-card companies, telephone calling-card numbers for all the long-distance carriers, and a host of computer passwords. According to the authorities, she shared her information with at least 150 other hackers across the country, and was directly responsible for an estimated $500,000 in losses. Her sentence was considered light by her victims.[16]

6

Pranksters and
Information Thieves

When Craig Neidorf was in elementary school he was a whiz at a video games. At thirteen he discovered computers. By age fourteen, under the handle "Knight Lightning," he was a wizard hacker—he knew computer networks as well as he knew his own neighborhood. At sixteen he and a friend started *Phrack*, a newsletter for hackers. (The name *Phrack* was a combination of the words *phreak* and *hack*.) *Phrack* was not mailed out in written form, but was published electronically through various bulletin boards. It was free.

In 1990, Neidorf was a prelaw student at the University of Missouri, and *Phrack* had become popular among phreaks and hackers nationwide. Then in Issue 24, Neidorf published a computer text file he had received from "The Prophet," a Legion of Doom member who read *Phrack* regularly and often corresponded with the editors. The file, titled, "Control Office Administration of Enhanced 911 Services for Special Services and Major

Account Centers," had been taken from BellSouth Telephone Company's computers.

The government was monitoring the activities of some members of the Legion of Doom, as part of a crackdown on hackers, when agents came across the E911 file in *Phrack*. Eventually, The Prophet and two other members of the Legion of Doom were charged with conspiracy, computer fraud, wire fraud, access device fraud, and interstate transportation of stolen property. They pled guilty to reduced charges and agreed to testify against Neidorf.

The federal government claimed that the publication of the E911 document in *Phrack* could allow hackers to seriously disrupt 911 emergency services. Neidorf was charged with ten felony counts of wire fraud, which carried a maximum penalty of sixty-five years in prison. He pled not guilty, and his trial began July 23, 1990.

Dorothy Denning, head of Georgetown University's computer science department, and John Nagle, a computer consultant in Menlo Park, California, were expert witnesses at Neidorf's trial. Both testified that a number of articles, reports, and books on the E911 system were easily available to anyone who wanted them, and that the document published in *Phrack* did not give away any secrets.

Four days after Neidorf's trial began, the government dropped all charges. Although the trial was over quickly, when it ended, Neidorf owed $100,000 in legal fees.[1]

Desiring Data

Why was an obscure, hard-to-read technical document worth stealing in the first place? Because the professed object of most hacking is to acquire information. Since electronic intruders never know which piece of information will prove useful, they simply browse files. When information is available for the taking, crackers may download technical manuals, user files, programs used to run a system, research notes, or anything else that looks interesting. The more remarkable the information appears, the more clever the hack, and thus the more hack value the deed has.

When a choice bit of data is captured, it's passed along to other hackers, to improve hacking skills or simply for brag value. Because, most hackers reason, what good is a great hack if no one knows you did it?

Gotcha!

Since hackers love to brag, many can't resist leaving a calling card behind when they crack a computer system. These messages were left when playful hackers broke into computers: Vocational-technical students in a computer programming class logged on and got the message, "Gotcha! This computer is stoned." Data was not lost, but classes had to be postponed while the gag program was located and erased. A university graduate student entered his file on the school's computer to review his research data and found a computer-generated picture of a nude at the end of the file. Corporate users of a voice-mail system have been harassed with recorded insults and profanity.

More elaborate pranks have resulted in substantial legal penalties for the intruder. For instance, on April 27, 1987, viewers of the Home Box Office (HBO) channel on cable television were watching *The Falcon and the Snowman* when their screen suddenly went blank. For the next four minutes, the following message appeared: "Good evening HBO from Captain Midnight. $12.95 a month? No way! (Show-time/Movie Channel, beware!)"

The prankster, a satellite dish salesman and electronic engineer, was quickly caught after he was overheard talking about his deed on a pay telephone. He told authorities the purpose of his act was to protest the scrambling of HBO's satellite signal. He was charged with transmitting without a license, sentenced to one year's probation, and fined $5,000.[2]

In another incident in June 1989, all calls to the Palm Beach County Probation Department in Delray Beach, Florida, were somehow answered by "Tina," a phone-sex employee in New York state. The prankster in this case, a sixteen-year-old hacker known as "Fry Guy," confessed when he was caught the following month.

The Tina caper was not Fry Guy's only transgression. He had allegedly helped steal $6,000 from Western Union and had committed credit-card fraud. Fry Guy was charged with eleven counts of computer fraud, unauthorized computer access, and wire fraud.[3]

While such pranks sometimes seem funny to outside observers, law enforcement officials take them seriously because of the potential for harm. Imagine dialing 911 to report a medical emergency, only to be connected to a phone-sex service. (Hackers have boasted that such a stunt is entirely possible.)

War Games

The movie *War Games* inspired many computer buffs when it came out in 1983. The star of the story, a teenage hacker, uses his home computer to try to break into the North American Air Defense Command (NORAD) system in Colorado. Eventually successful, he blunders into a situation that poises the United States on the brink of World War III.

The film's popularity led to much editorializing about hackers. Could one teenage wizard actually plunge the country into a war? Was hacking a serious threat, or simply a minor annoyance blown out of proportion by one Hollywood production? Should hackers be punished as criminals? If so, how stiff should penalties be?

The questions remain unanswered. But the fascination with breaking into military computers continues.

Military installations like NORAD are often targets for computer users who see hack value in breaking into such forbidden fruits on the network. In June 1989, a fourteen-year-old Kansas boy used his computer to crack a U.S. Air Force satellite-positioning system. He had become expert at breaking into a certain type of computer, and in addition to military agencies, wandered through the files of at least two hundred companies. "It's just a matter of getting the right passwords," the boy told investigators.

Typical of most hackers, the Kansas wizard kept track of his exploits in a personal journal, which proved a handy index for police investigators.[4]

An eighteen-year-old Israeli youth was charged in 1991 with breaking into a Pentagon computer during Operation Desert Storm. Reports from an Israeli newspaper indicated that the youth had read secret information on the Patriot missile.[5]

Software Piracy

Stealing information in the form of software is also illegal. It is legal for bulletin boards and user groups to offer members shareware or public domain software, but making copies of commercial software, for re-sale or to give to others, is a crime. Making one backup copy of purchased software is recommended, but additional copies are illegal without the permission of the software publisher. It is also illegal for companies, schools, or other organizations with many machines to buy one copy of a program, then make additional copies for use in all their computers.

Former U.S. President George Bush signed a bill in 1992 to make commercial software piracy a felony, punishable by up to five years in prison, and fines of up to $250,000, for anyone convicted of stealing at least ten copies of a program or more then $2,500 worth of software.

Although software is covered by the 1980 Computer Software Copyright Act, software piracy has been called a major growth industry in the United States. The Software Publishers Association (SPA) estimates that bootlegging results in a loss of $1.2 billion to American software publishers each year. The organization claims that one in five personal computer programs in use today is an illegal copy. Lotus, Inc., says that over one-half of the sales of Lotus 1-2-3, a commercial accounting program, are lost to pirates—approximately $160 million in lost sales a year. MicroPro estimates there are two to three illegal copies of WordStar, a word processing program, for every copy sold.[6]

In July 1992, Joshua Quittner, a reporter for New York's *Newsday*, interviewed "Ice Man" and "Maniac," two teenage members of the group Micro Pirates Incorporated. In response to Quittner's question, "Are you software pirates, too?" Ice Man said, "Software piracy is, in the computer underground, the biggest thing. There are [international] groups like The Humble Guys (THG) and International Network of Crackers (INC), run by fourteen- and fifteen-year-olds. They have people who work in companies, and they'll take the software and crack it—the software protection—and then distribute it."[7]

Most experienced hackers know other hackers who abuse their knowledge, as in the following incidents: Two teenagers in New York hack a bank's computer, steal credit-card numbers, then try to order over $1,000 in computer equipment.[8] A hacker in Great Britain breaks into the electronic mailbox for His Royal Highness, Prince Philip, and leaves the message, "I do so enjoy puzzles and games. Ta. Ta. Pip! Pip!"[9] Someone in Illinois gains access to a university's computers, then alters grades, falsifies a transcript, and enrolls students in courses for which they hadn't paid.[10]

High-tech data diddling, whether intended as a prank, as a trophy of a successful hack, or as retribution, is many times clever, funny, and daring, at first glance. But whenever a hacker slips over the line and changes electronically stored information belonging to someone else, or uses information to cause damage, either intentionally or unintentionally, that person risks legal prosecution.

7

Darkside Hacking

When he was arrested in December 1988, Kevin Mitnick, twenty-five, was declared "a very, very great danger to the community," and denied bail by U.S. District Judge Mariana Pfaelzer. While in jail, Mitnick was not allowed access to a telephone, except to call his wife, mother, or lawyer. In fact, giving him a telephone was compared to giving a gun to a hit man.

Was Mitnick a serial killer? An armed robber?

No—Mitnick was a programmer with a history of vicious computer capers. At seventeen he cracked Pacific Bell Telephone's computer system and stole technical data. Later he was accused of breaking into computers at several locations in the United States and at the University of Leeds in England in order to steal valuable programs and long-distance telephone services.

Mitnick was considered doubly dangerous because of his apparent appetite for electronic revenge. After Mitnick served six months in a juvenile detention center for the Pacific Bell incident, the sentencing judge found his credit information altered, and the telephone of a probation officer involved in the case was mysteriously disconnected. The records of Mitznick's crimes somehow vanished from police computers. He was once suspected of damaging a company that had refused him a job by planting a false story on a financial news network.

Mitnick was convicted of computer fraud in January 1989, and sentenced to one year in prison. Because his attorney convinced the court that Mitnick was addicted to computers, the jail term was followed by six months in a rehabilitation program.[1]

According to Katie Hafner and John Markoff, authors of *Cyberpunk—Outlaws and Hackers on the Computer Frontier,* Kevin Mitnik served his sentence in a Federal prison in Southern California. After his release from jail, Mitnick completed a rehabilitation program patterned after the twelve-step treatment model for Alcoholics Anonymous. He was finally allowed to seek work as a computer operator, and was eventually hired as a programmer for a health-care provider in the Los Angeles area.[2]

Intentional Damage

While most hackers claim curiosity and a desire to learn as motives for cracking computer systems, a few "darkside" hackers seem drawn to computing as a means to do harm to others. For these individuals, computers are convenient instruments of malice.

One such darkside hacker, a California computer security employee known on-line as "Dark Dante," was tracked for a year by the FBI. His identity was so well publicized that he was finally turned in by checkers in the supermarket where he shopped. He was charged with running a computer crime ring that invaded the Army's MASNET computer network to get information used in an FBI investigation of former Philippine President Ferdinand Marcos. Dark Dante and other members of his group were also accused of purloining secret flight orders for thousands of Army paratroopers on maneuvers in North Carolina, and stealing the access code for the Soviet Consulate in San Francisco.[3]

"Susan Thunder" (her on-line name), another California hacker, once worked with Kevin Mitnick. In 1983 she told a U.S. Senate Subcommittee how she and her friends used their personal computers to alter victims' credit ratings and insert obscenities. The group had also attempted to shut down the entire California telephone system.[4]

Darkside hackers often access the information inside computers for revenge.

Newsweek reporter Richard Sandza learned how far malicious hackers would go a few years ago when he wrote an article about hackers. To learn about the hacker underground and bulletin board systems, he went undercover as "Montana Wildhack," earning the trust of hackers he met on-line. After his story was published, Sandza received hundreds of harassing phone calls from hackers, his life was threatened, and his credit-card numbers were traded across the United States.[5]

Revenge is also a powerful motive for employees or ex-employees with computer knowledge and a flexible conscience, if they believe an employer has treated them unfairly. In Chicago in 1986, a disgruntled employee who had been laid off by Encyclopaedia Britannica entered the company's data base and made changes in the text for the new edition. "Jesus Christ" became "Allah," for example, and the names of company executives were inserted in odd places.[6]

Donald Gene Burleson was fired as a programmer for a Texas insurance brokerage firm in 1985. Two days later he got even. Burleson placed in the company's computer system a rogue program that was set to wipe out all records of sales commissions once each month. As a result, before the program was defused, the company lost 168,000 payroll records and paychecks were delayed for a month. Burleson was caught when another employee reported seeing him at a computer terminal after he was supposed to have left the company.[7]

Sometimes rival hacker groups use their skills in feuds with each other. In December of 1992, activities of a hacker group in the New York City area that led to the arrest of two members may have been the result of revenge-by-computer. Members of the New York group, the Masters of Deception, allegedly used their computers and modems to change phone services and otherwise annoy members of the Legion of Doom, a Texas-based group. The rivalry between the two groups supposedly started when a Legion of Doom member published belittling remarks about MOD in a computer journal.[8]

Unintentional Damage

When hackers erase data files to cover their tracks after a break-in, they can do unexpected damage that they cannot repair. In an interview with a *New York Times* reporter after being caught by the FBI, a member of a group of Wisconsin teenagers who called themselves the 414s (after their local telephone area code) admitted to incorrectly erasing a file in a computer at the Sloan-Kettering Cancer Center in New York. This incident was particularly frightening, since radiation therapy exposure times and dosages for cancer patients undergoing X-ray therapy were among the files kept on the center's computer.

The same group allegedly compromised computer files at the nuclear weapons research facility at Los Alamos, New Mexico.[9]

Electronic Spies

Espionage is another destructive venture that may appeal to darkside hackers operating on the wrong side of the law.

The most famous case of computer espionage to date is detailed in *The Cuckoo's Egg,* by Clifford Stoll. In 1986, Stoll was an astrophysicist/computer expert who had just been hired as a systems administrator for the mainframe computers at Lawrence Berkeley Laboratory in California. When a seventy-five cent accounting error showed up, Stoll was asked to check it out. In the process, he discovered that a network intruder had been using the account of a scientist who had left the laboratory.

Stoll focused his ample energy and enthusiasm on tracking the hacker. He wrote programs that would alert him every time the culprit logged on, and he eventually enlisted the help of the FBI and other government officials, both in the United States and in Germany.

After several months, Stoll's diligence paid off. The break-ins were traced to a group of West German hackers called Chaos, who were breaking into computers on the Internet network, stealing military data, and selling it to the Soviet KGB. Peter Carl, Markus Hess, and Dirk-Otto Brzezinski (also known as Dob) were indicted on espionage charges. Robert Anton Wilson, a fourth suspect, died mysteriously before he could be arrested.

The case finally came to trial in January 1990. Carl was sentenced to two years in prison and fined 3,000 marks ($1500). Hess was sentenced to one year and eight months, and fined 10,000 marks. Dob received a sentence of one year and two months and a 5,000-mark fine.[10]

In a more recent episode, Dutch teenagers reportedly gained access to U.S. Defense Department computers during the Persian Gulf war and changed or copied unclassified but highly sensitive information. At a hearing of the Senate Governmental Affairs subcommittee on government information, Jack L. Brock, Jr., director of the General Accounting Office's government information division, testified that between April 1990 and May 1991, the hackers penetrated Army, Navy, and Air Force computer systems at thirty-four sites. Once inside the computers, the intruders read crucial data on military personnel, the type and amount of military equipment being moved to the gulf, missile targeting, and the development of important weapons systems. Evidence also indicated that hackers were looking for information about nuclear weapons.[11]

Darkside hackers are determined to use their skills in ways contrived to cause the most harm. It is not surprising, then, that, because of the damage such acts can do, the antisocial and criminal behavior of darkside hackers has been called electronic terrorism.

8

Viruses, Worms and Other Sinister Programs

There are more than 1,200 bugs out there, and the infections they spread put their victims out of action until the healing process begins. This may sound like a description of the common cold or influenza virus, except that the "virus" referred to here doesn't attack people. This bug is made by human hands, and it attacks linked computers. It's spread by shared software almost as easily as a sneeze, and the illness it causes can be every bit as weakening as the flu.

Michelangelo

Around the world on March 6, 1992, computer users reported for work, booted up their machines, and waited for the log-on sequence to begin. But instead of the normal buzz and whir of healthy disk drives, a few operators heard a sickening clunk, clunk, clunk. Then the machines "crashed." "Nothing worked," one legal secretary said later.

Many computer operators who had been reading the newspapers prior to that day were able to find and kill the bug before it could do damage. Weeks before the sixth of March, word had spread about a computer virus discovered by a German scientist in April, 1991. Dubbed Michelangelo, because it was set to go off on the artist's 517th birthday, the virus had spread rapidly among IBM microcomputers and IBM clones. Those who heeded these prior warnings were able to protect themselves, either by not turning their computers on until after the sixth, thus bypassing March 6 on their computers' internal calendars, or by running "vaccine" programs designed to detect and cure viruses.[1]

Michelangelo's origins were uncertain. It was commonly believed that the virus was written in Sweden or the Netherlands, and traveled to other countries in infected software. Like all computer viruses, Michelangelo was able to copy itself endlessly onto host fixed and floppy disks. The infection spread by the virus caused the sick machines to erase data stored on hard disks and floppy disks. The logic bomb ingredient of the virus told it to do its damage on March 6.

When the casualties of Michelangelo were added up, it was not the raging epidemic many had feared. However, experts estimated that at least 10,000 computers were hit worldwide. And the virus did strike a dozen companies in the United States, including the New York City subway system and the Wall Street brokerage firm Drexel Burnham Lambert. In Germany, eighty business computers were infected. In Great Britain, where Scotland Yard's Computer Crime Unit monitored the virus, only one incident was reported. An architectural and civil engineering firm in Japan lost $20,000 to $30,000 worth of data, including architectural drawings. South Africa was the hardest hit, reporting 1,000 computers in 500 companies disabled.[2]

Though publicity about the virus has faded, if it remains undetected, the Michelangelo virus can lie in wait inside a computer, to come alive again and erase hard disks on March 6 of any year.

How Viruses Work

Computer viruses have the following traits in common:
- They are self-duplicating.
- They are specific to one kind of computer, such as IBM or Macintosh PCs.
- They are spread by shared disks, or over telephone lines via modems.
- The virus is activated by running, accidentally, the computer code in which it is embedded. It can be activated by a trigger, such as a date, time, or command word.
- They are difficult to trace.

According to the Computer Virus Industry Association, there are three classes of viruses: boot infectors, system infectors, and general executable program infectors.

Boot infectors attach themselves to that section of a floppy or hard disk that lets the user "boot up" to begin working with the computer. When one of these viruses, like Michelangelo, is in place, it gains control as the computer is first turned on by moving from the boot sector of the floppy disk into the computer's memory.

The virus can then infect the hard disk. At this point, any new disk placed in the floppy disk drive can also become infected.

System infectors gain control after the computer is booted up. They enter operating system files, such as the MS-DOS files, COPY, DIR, and ERASE. They can be set to activate at a given time, or they can begin messing up computer operations right away, by increasing the time taken to perform functions, scrambling data, or erasing files.

General executable program infectors are the most dangerous type of virus, since they can spread to any program in a system. For example, games, spreadsheets, and word processing and utility programs are all vulnerable.

The results of a virus infection can be harmless or deadly. Some viruses are simply intended to be funny. One displays the message "Gotcha," then self-destructs. Another is called the "Cookie Monster." It flashes the message, "I want a cookie," on the screen, and users must "feed" the word *cookie* to the monster to keep it under control. The "Stoned" virus flashes a message calling for the legalization of marijuana.

Most viruses are not so harmless, however. A few infamous viruses have been around for several years. The Pakistani Brain is a boot sector infector which originated in pirated disks. An especially deadly virus called the Disk Killer erases everything on the hard disk. Equally scary is the Mutation Engine, an Eastern European creation that can be modified to commit a harmless joke or erase everything. This virus is doubly toxic, because it is almost undetectable.[3]

Fortunately, sometimes a potentially deadly virus is disabled before it can do its damage. A virus called Friday the 13th, for example, was designed to wipe out files on Friday, May 13, 1988, the fortieth anniversary of the last day Palestine existed as a political entity. But before the Friday the 13th virus could activate, Yuval Rakavy, a student at Hebrew University, discovered and defused the virus code.

Other Sinister Programs

Some infectious computer programs are less deadly than the virus. For example, a *worm*, Robert Tappan Morris' toxin of choice, reproduces itself, as does a virus, and can load up a system's memory, causing it to crash, but it does not usually destroy data.

Several other nuisance programs also differ from viruses, in that they do not reproduce themselves. The *Trojan horse* type, for instance, is named for the fabled giant wooden horse in which Greek warriors were smuggled into Troy. True to its name, this program is disguised as an innocent code, but it has a hidden purpose.

Members of the Inner Circle hackers' group used a Trojan horse concealed in a chess game to gain entry to a Canadian mainframe computer they had been trying to crack. They talked the system operator into playing the game with them, then, while the chess program was running, it opened a powerful, unauthorized account in the host computer for the hackers to use later, undetected.[4]

Computer consultant Leonard Rose, Jr., a.k.a. "Terminus," of Middletown, Maryland, also allegedly used a Trojan horse program to alter stolen AT&T software. After his arrest in 1990, prosecutors claimed that the programming changes Rose made would allow hackers to gain secret access to computer systems using the AT&T UNIX software, and to learn passwords used on the system. Rose pled guilty to wire fraud and was sentenced to one year in prison.[5]

The *logic bomb* or *time bomb* is similar to a Trojan horse, but it is programmed to go off at a particular time. Logic bombs are the favorite device of angry employees intent on getting even, because they can plant such a program and set it to go off and do damage sometime after they leave the company.

In 1985, an employee fired from Minnesota Tipboard Company planted a time bomb that would erase sensitive information and files. Unless the company paid him $350 a week while he hunted for another job, he said, he would trigger the bomb. The company hired security experts who found and defused the bomb, and the ex-employee was arrested for extortion.[6]

Trapdoors Can Let Intruders In

Trapdoors may allow intruders to penetrate a system, but they are not always created for the purpose of causing damage. They are sometimes legitimate lines of code that are written into programs by programmers to provide an easy entrance for maintenance. However, if the trapdoor is not closed after its purpose has been served, browsing hackers can discover the hidden code. The hackers can then gain unauthorized access by using the trapdoor to skirt normal security procedures.

During a dispute over payment in 1990, Logisticon, Inc., a software company, deliberately used a trapdoor to impair a program the company had sold to Revlon. Logisticon's action crippled a major Revlon distribution center for three days.[7]

Virus Control

A *vaccine* is an antiviral program especially written to find a virus hidden in a computer's operating system. Scanning antiviral software checks a program or disk for virus code. Better programs scan for two hundred or more known viruses and are updated frequently, but all scan programs operate after the virus has already copied itself. A few can erase the virus, but most only scan then tell the user where to get help if one is found.

Memory-resident antiviral software checks out each program before it loads, then prevents foreign code from running. These vaccines work before the virus has a chance to duplicate itself inside an infected computer.

There are a wide range of virus protection programs on the market, and some are offered free or at low cost by virus experts and consultants.

Once a virus is detected, it can take an expert programmer many hours—at great expense—to pinpoint and get rid of it. When a virus can be traced to its originator, that person faces prosecution for illegal computer activity.

Two months after Michelangelo struck, two Cornell University students learned this fact the hard way. They were arrested for creating a virus called MBDF-A. The two allegedly planted the virus in three Macintosh computer games that they offered to others via telephone link, and it infected all the computers that ran the program. When players in the U.S., Great Britain, and Japan used the games, the virus wiped out operating programs. Since the virus caused total damages of more than $1,000, the two students faced felony charges, punishable by a maximum of four years in prison.[8]

An Apple a Day . . .

Since the best treatment for any disease is prevention, experts offer several tips for safe computing to guard against virus infection:

- Use reliable sources for programs. Shareware and public domain software posted for the taking on bulletin boards are most likely to be infected, so computer users who trade programs should be careful. Pirated copies of software can also pass along a virus infection. Purchased programs in shrinkwrap are most likely to be virus-free, but there have been exceptions.
- Write-protect all the disks used, so no one can transmit a virus to them.
- If the system in use has a hard or fixed disk, never boot from a diskette.
- Make backup copies frequently.
- Watch for changes in the way a system works. Do programs take longer than usual to load? Do disk access times seem excessively long for the task to be performed? Are there unusual error messages? Is less system memory available than usual? Have programs or files mysteriously disappeared?

Has available disk space been suddenly reduced? The presence of any one of these "symptoms" can indicate the presence of a virus.

- Use a reliable antivirus program regularly to scan for viruses.

When a virus is detected, it is important to tell others who might have used the same disks, in order to prevent further spread of the infection. Unfortunately, the only way a computer can be made completely safe from virus infection is to isolate the machine and never allow it to run shared disks or public domain software.

The motive for creating a virus or other destructive program may be simply to show off one's programming expertise, but the deadly bugs are also used as instruments of extortion or revenge. Experts have compared the planting of viruses to such crimes as "putting typhoid in the public water supply," or "picking up a baseball bat to break windows, instead of hitting balls." Whatever the motive, victims of these attacks agree that the destruction caused hardly justifies the few moments of satisfaction a virus's creator feels when he or she first knows the program will work.

9

Laws and Civil Liberties in Cyberspace

In 1990 hackers came under siege. From Arizona to Texas to New York, on May 7, 8, and 9 of that year, 150 Secret Service and police officers staged surprise raids in 14 American cities. Armed with guns and more than twenty search warrants, the officers seized 42 computers and 23,000 disks. They also shut down twenty-five electronic bulletin boards. The target of this roundup, dubbed "Operation Sundevil," was a group of youthful hackers, many of them members of the Legion of Doom, suspected of trafficking in stolen credit-card numbers, telephone access codes, and other illegally obtained electronic information.

The first successful prosecution to result from the raid took place in February 1992, when Robert Chandler, twenty-one, pled guilty in federal court in California to a felony, possessing fifteen or more telephone access codes. According to Scott Charney, head of the Justice Department's computer crime unit in

Washington, D.C., Chandler admitted to using the access codes to make toll-free long-distance telephone calls.[1]

Two months before the Operation Sundevil arrests, on March 1, 1990, the Austin, Texas, offices of Steve Jackson Games, a publisher of noncomputerized, Dungeons-and-Dragons-type "adventure" games, were raided by the U.S. Secret Service. Although Jackson's games were marketed as printed rule books and were not sold on computer disks, the agents took computers, laser printers, and photocopy machines, as well as disks containing work in progress.

Apparently Jackson's games business was targeted because two of his employees were under investigation for hacker activities related to the *Phrack*/E911 incident. Also of interest to agents was a new game in progress, "GURPS (Generic Universal Role Playing System) Cyberpunk," which one government agent had referred to as a "handbook on computer crime."

In defense of the material his company produced, Jackson later told *The Futurist*, "There is far less technical information in this game than in *2600 Magazine*" (a hacker's journal).[2]

Who Owns Cyberspace?

Law enforcement authorities wanted the 1990 raids to send the message that computer crime doesn't pay. Many hackers and would-be hackers probably got the message, but the ambitious dragnet also raised disturbing constitutional issues. Were the electronic bulletin boards shut down in the raid as entitled to protection under the

First Amendment as the words on a printed page? When computers and disks were seized, were citizens deprived of "life, liberty, or property, without due process of law," as prohibited by the Fourteenth Amendment?

After news of the raids was broadcast, more questions were raised. How can citizens protect their privacy when every telephone call, credit-card charge, and cash-card transaction is recorded electronically? Who owns such information? What happens to property rights when documents can be digitally reproduced that are exactly like the original? Should electronic signals be subject to special laws created especially for cyberspace?

As the questions multiplied, concerned individuals debated answers on bulletin boards, person-to-person, on-line, and at conferences and conventions. Computer ethics and the law became the focus of attention across the United States and around the world.

Hackers' Conferences

In August 1989, an international meeting of hackers was held in Amsterdam, the Netherlands. Also in 1989, two hundred hackers gathered in California for the fifth annual Hackers' Conference to discuss "Forbidden Knowledge in a Technological Society," as well as ways to improve the hacker image.

At the conference in Amsterdam, a code of behavior for hackers had been drawn up. Many of those in attendance in California agreed that hackers need to monitor their activities. Hackers "have to come out of the closet," one person at the California conference said. "We need to talk about how what we do is useful and how it can be dangerous."[3]

Computer buffs met in Amsterdam again in August of 1993, for the Hackers at the End of the Universe conference. The organizer, a Dutch computer magazine called *Hack-Tic*, said the conference was intended for "hackers, phone phreaks, programmers, computer haters, data travelers, electro-wizards, networkers, hardware freaks, techno-anarchists, communications junkies, cyberpunks, system managers, stupid users, paranoid androids, Unix gurus, whizz kids, warez dudes, law-enforcement officers, guerrilla heating engineers and other assorted bald, long-haired or unshaven scum."[4]

At one session of the conference, "Networking for the Masses," participants discussed using information from computers to fight government oppression. Another popular topic was how hackers could help protect privacy by pushing for more secure codes.

Hacker ethics was the topic of concern for the First Conference on Computers, Freedom, and Privacy, sponsored in March, 1991, by Computer Professionals for Social Responsibility (CPSR), a group of computer professionals dedicated to promoting ethics in computing. The weekend event drew FBI and Secret Service agents, lawyers, privacy advocates, computer professionals, educators, hackers, and other interested parties to the San Francisco Bay area to listen to formal speeches and to debate the issues.

A second CPSR-sponsored conference convened in Washington, D.C., in 1992.

CFP '93, the Third Conference on Computers, Freedom, and Privacy, met March 9–12, 1993, in

Burlingame, California. According to Jay Thorwaldson, who attended the conference and was the media coordinator for CFP '93, cryptography was a hot topic in 1993.

Cryptography, as applied to computer and telephone users, involves encrypting—putting into code—computer transmissions and phone conversations through use of a Data Encryption Standard (DES) chip. The National Security Agency designed such a system in the 1970s with IBM, but it has yet to be put into use because of controversy over who should get the decode key. Since wiretaps don't work on a DES-encrypted phone, the government is pushing to impose a universal encryption standard on telecommunications manufacturers for which only the government would hold the key.[5]

In the debate at CFP '93, "on the side of total privacy and total security were the libertarians," says Thorwaldson. "On the other side of the issue is where law enforcement comes in. If you have totally secure cryptography, inviolable even from legitimate court order or wiretaps, you can get material on-line, but you can't de-crypt it. Then, you have a completely secure communications channel for criminal activity. That's not acceptable to national security people, or to law enforcement."

At CFP '93, Dorothy Denning, head of the computer science department at Georgetown University, proposed a compromise, whereby everyone who sends or receives a coded message on-line would have a public and a private key. As Thorwaldson explains the proposal: "Everybody gets to know your public key, and they can send you messages encrypted in your public key. You could use it with any encryption standard. You get this garbly message, then only you have the private key to

90

unlock the message being sent to you. The material encrypted and sent to you on the network is completely secure.

"That freaks out a lot of people," Thorwaldson continues. "Dorothy Denning proposed that there be some kind of electronic Fort Knox, for everyone's private key. So if somebody like the FBI decides that Jay Thorwaldson is engaged in criminal activity, they can get a court order and go to this repository where Thorwaldson keeps his private key (copy of his code). They can then get that code, and get all my material out of my computer."[6]

Clearly, cryptography is another telecommunications issue that will not be quickly resolved.

27th Amendment for High Tech?

At the First Conference on Computers, Freedom, and Privacy, Laurence Tribe, a Harvard University professor of constitutional law introduced his proposal for a 27th amendment to the United States Constitution. The amendment is needed, he claimed, to protect the right of computer users to communicate freely and privately, and to protect all citizens from having their private data collected and shared without their express approval.

The problem, Tribe said, is that the courts do not interpret the Constitution the same way each time, when they apply its provisions to cases involving high technology. His proposed amendment states that the freedoms in the Bill of Rights "shall be construed as fully applicable without regard to the technological method or medium through which information content is generated, stored, altered or controlled." Critics of Tribe's proposal argue that the Constitution already protects civil liberties as applied to new technologies.[7]

The Electronic Freedom Foundation

The rise in anxiety levels caused by the government-regulation-versus-hackers'-rights issue led to the formation of the Electronic Freedom Foundation (EFF). The foundation was started in June, 1990, by three concerned individuals: John Perry Barlow, songwriter for the Grateful Dead and computer wizard; Mitch Kapor, creator of the Lotus 1-2-3 spreadsheet and Lotus Development Corporation; and Steven Wozniak, Apple Computer Inc. co-founder. In Barlow's words, the EFF will "raise and disburse funds for education, lobbying, and litigation in the areas relating to digital speech and the extension of the Constitution into Cyberspace."[8]

The EFF funded Steve Jackson's legal battle and has filed suit against the federal government to establish constitutional limits on the search and seizure of computers, bulletin board systems, books, and manuscripts at Steve Jackson Games.

However, EFF co-founder Kapor has often said that the EFF is not simply a "hackers' defense fund." "We don't see our mission as defending people who illegally enter computer systems," he told the *Chicago Tribune* in 1990.[9]

The Importance of Computer Security

One point that hackers, law enforcement officials, businesspersons, computer professionals, and educators agree on is that computer systems with excellent security are the least likely to be cracked. Yet, experts claim that too many computer owners and users do not pay enough attention to security:

- "Given that almost everyone is aware of the existence and capabilities of hackers—and aware of how others can go through the doors hackers open—the total lack of security in the world's computers is shocking."—Chris Goggans, *Computerworld*.[10]

- "At many companies, the only security system is a poster above the copy machine that shows a dog with a moustache and a Sherlock Holmes hat."—David Stang, chairman of the International Computer Security Association, Washington, D.C.[11]

- "We build computer rooms that have physical security around them, but we forget about the telecommunications ports in the backs of these machines. They are an important part of how the machines communicate, but they are also a point of easy access. It's like building Fort Knox, and leaving the entire back side of the vault and fence off, if you don't put security around your computer's telecommunications port."—Harold Hendershot, Supervisory Special Agent, Computer Fraud and Abuse Program, Federal Bureau of Investigation.[12]

- "America's increasingly computerized society will become dangerously vulnerable to attacks by criminals and high-tech terrorists unless new nationwide computer security precautions are taken soon."—*The Washington Post*, summing up a 1990 report by the National Research Council, titled "Computers at Risk."[13]

Passwords, Smartcards, Keys, and Other High Tech Locks

Passwords can be the first step toward locking out unauthorized computer users, but they are also often the weakest link in the security chain. For example, when a computer is shared by many users, accounts are assigned by name. Account names need not be kept secret, but the password that allows users to log on and begin using the accounts should be known only to those users.

"People don't understand how critical passwords are," says Purdue University's computer security expert, Eugene Spafford. "So they are not as creative in picking them as they should be." (One reformed cracker who now helps others with computer security says he was successful in three tries the first time he tried to break into a system by guessing the password.)

Obvious passwords that are easily guessed by would-be intruders include the user's name ("Sue," "Tom," "John"), birthdays, nicknames, and other obvious choices. At Purdue, for example, says Spafford, "It's a sure bet some student or faculty among our 10,000 computer users will use as a password the word, 'Purdue,' "Eudrup' (Purdue spelled backwards), or 'Boilermaker.' Those are words that users can remember.

"But often the words that pop into mind first are very high on the list of words somebody else would search for," Spafford adds. "[Hackers] simply take an on-line dictionary of words, and try every word, one after the other, to see if one is a password. Depending on user population, there's a good chance that one user somewhere will have one of these weak passwords."[14]

Choose a set of random characters for a password, such as *(?SOV#!, advise the experts, and don't post the password in an obvious place near the computer workstation, or on the bulletin board in the hall. Passwords should be changed often, and default passwords, given to all new accounts on a system, should not be used. And never, never use the account name as the password.

In addition to passwords, access to a computer can be limited by physically locking up the machine, by issuing magnetic "smart cards" that must be used to gain access, or by using a physical trait to identify the operator. Passwords can be discovered, keys can be copied, and cards can be stolen, but biological identification is hard for an intruder to bypass.

Since no two individuals have the same signature, or the same fingerprints, these are two traits that may be used to identify a legitimate computer user. The pattern of blood vessels in the eye, and the vibration of the voice are also personal identifying features that can be checked by a computer before allowing access.

Other guards that may be posted at the gates include modems that call the user back before allowing entry to the system, log-on records, and encryption devices.

"Most sites keep records of who has been logging onto a system," says Kenneth van Wyk, technical coordinator for the Software Engineering Institute, Computer Emergency Response Team (CERT) at Carnegie Mellon University. "They can also keep track of every program a person runs. A system administrator that monitors those audit logs and looks for abnormalities might say, 'Wait a minute, my janitor's logged on from Paris.' That's the sort of thing that might clue somebody off to do further investigating."[15]

Encryption hardware or software does not keep users out, but it does limit access to information by scrambling data to make it unreadable. A key must be used to descramble the material so it can be read.

Some of the above security measures are relatively inexpensive and easy to use, while others, such as smart cards and encryption devices, can be complicated and expensive. System owners must decide the value of their stored data, then choose a security system that will do the desired job for the money spent.

But if computer owners want the security job done right, says Spafford, a full-time security person should be assigned. In locations where break-ins have been a problem, "there is usually nobody in charge who knows what is going on. And there may be no well established procedures for everybody to know how the system is supposed to be used."

The person running a computer should also pay close attention to the machine's behavior, Spafford adds. Is an account being heavily used? Are there logged messages that someone is exceeding authorization? "Most systems have the capability to store and present that information," he says. "But often the people running the systems don't turn it on, or don't read it because it's a chore. If they did, they might discover things early on."

On-Line Ethics

Using the system correctly includes knowing and heeding user responsibilities. Many organizations for computer professionals now have written codes of ethics that members are expected to follow. For example, the Association for Computing Machinery (ACM), the Institute of Electrical and Electronics Engineers (IEEE), the Data Processing Management Association (DPMA) and the International Federation for Information Processing (IFIP) all have a professional code of ethics.

Scott Charney, chief of the Computer Crime Unit for the U.S. Department of Justice, believes more schools should include ethics in the computer science curriculum. "Many high schools teach driver's education," he illustrates, "and they don't put students in cars without teaching the rules of the road. But we give kids computers and say, go out and have fun. The dramatic impact is not as noticeable drivers can hit someone with a car and kill them. But computer users can still do a lot of damage."

It is difficult in the nameless, faceless forum computers provide to demand accountability, says Charney, but using "social mores" may help. "For example, if you ostracize a 'flamer'—someone who is abusing [computer] bulletin board privileges by being obnoxious or outrageous—that is fairly effective."[16]

Purdue's Eugene Spafford compares today's ethical dilemma in computing to use of the telephone. "In the beginning, everybody was on a party line. Telephones were the town entertainment, and everybody listened in. Then people realized that this wasn't very nice. We developed a tradition, an etiquette about how to use the phone. Laws followed, to help regulate who could do what with the telephone. We're at the same stage now with computers. We need to develop the manners and the responsibility to go along with the freedoms."

Hackers as Heroes

Some hackers who once considered breaking into others' computer systems a fun pastime are now using their skills to help catch crackers and phreaks. Members of hacker groups have helped system operators trace trespassers and close gaps in the system that let crackers in. For instance, a hacker called "Control-C," caught trespassing inside Michigan Bell's computers, went to work for the company as a security and break-in expert; he became a feared opponent of hackers bent on illegal acts.

In his book, *Out of the Inner Circle,* "The Cracker" tells how a clever systems operator might persuade a hacker to reveal how he or she got into a system, and how a good computer security system can keep vandals and crackers out. He also admits: "I've come to realize that browsing raises some legal and ethical questions, such as: What constitutes invasion of privacy? What are the rights and privileges of the individuals involved? On a more technical level, to what degree are computer memory and electronically coded data entitled to protection under the law?"[17]

Across the country, student computer wizards are volunteering their time and expertise. In some states, computer science students from participating universities have volunteered to be matched with individuals who need help with a computing problem. For example, through its Nonprofit Computer Consultants program, the Development and Technical Assistance Center (DATA), based in New Haven, Connecticut, sends student computer gurus out to counsel nonprofit organizations in the community who have called in requesting technical help. The group charges small, sliding-scale fees for its mentor-matching services. The organization helps other interested colleges establish computer mentor clubs on campus.

The New Haven campus computer mentor program is modeled on the CompuMentor Project of San Francisco. Apple Computers, Inc., supports similar compumentor-type programs.

Locking the Doors

"Does developing more computer security mean freedoms to get into and out of computer systems will be impinged?" asks Harold Hendershot, special agent with the FBI's Computer Fraud and Abuse Program. "Yes, it does. But just as businesses had to begin locking doors, installing surveillance cameras, and hiring security guards when crime got worse after the 1950s, we now have to pay more attention to locking out computer criminals."[18]

Computer networks are often compared to neighborhoods and small communities. Just as cities and towns are tied together by streets, roads, and interstate highways, computers are linked through local, regional, and national networks. And just as neighborhood residents react to criminal activity by locking the doors to their houses, computer networks are now threatened by intruders and must develop a system of protection.

We have begun to more carefully guard entry to computer systems. But we must continue to be concerned that in locking out computer criminals, we do not sacrifice personal freedoms or give up the easy access that has made the networks a cooperative global neighborhood.

10

Citizens in Cyberspace

In *The Hacker Crackdown*, Bruce Sterling quotes from "The Conscience of a Hacker," by "The Mentor," as published in the electronic journal *Phrack* (Volume 1, Issue 7, Phile 3): "I made a discovery today. I found a computer. Wait a second, this is cool. It does what I want it to. If it makes a mistake, it's because I screwed it up. Not because it doesn't like me . . .

"And then it happened . . . a door opened to a world. . . . This is it . . . this is where I belong . . . the world of the electron and the switch, the beauty of the baud . . ."[1]

As increasing numbers of young persons discover the joys of computing, questions about laws and ethics in cyberspace will continue to multiply. Answers won't be any easier to find. But issues can become less divisive, if laws are updated to keep up with change, and if attitudes toward computer use and abuse reflect responsibility and concern for the rights of others.

When a person is arrested for a computer crime, all of the equipment pictured here—and more—may be seized as evidence. Included in the photo are a personal computer with hard disk, monitor, keyboard, and laser printer. (The computer has an internal modem.) Also shown are a facsimile (FAX) machine (far left), telephone answering machine, and a cordless telephone.

Updating the Law

Law enforcement agencies are already calling for changes in the 1986 Computer Fraud and Abuse Act. "The statute relies upon unauthorized access as the key to illegality," the U.S. Justice Department's Scott Charney points out, "and that doesn't always work. We've had cases, for example, where individuals have mailed viruses or other destructive code to someone else. That person then, as a dupe, unknowingly puts the virus into his or her machine. It's difficult to prove that the person who created the virus accessed the victim's machine. They didn't. We should be looking at unauthorized *use*, instead. Then it doesn't matter who touched the machine; what matters is what they did to the machine."

Secondly, says Charney, legislation to cover viruses should be passed, since the current law does not always apply to viruses and other malicious codes.

"And we need a forfeiture provision," Charney adds. "If someone is using their computer to attack other people, we should be able to take that computer away, because it is like any other weapon." Currently, electronic equipment can be seized in computer crime arrests, but it must be returned after its use as evidence has been served.

Finally, Charney recommends changes in the current law's sentencing provisions. "The way the original act was drafted, if you commit a computer crime under one of the subsections, then commit a second crime under a different subsection, you are not considered a second time offender." Since second-time offenders can be given stiffer penalties when convicted, Charney recommends that the law be clarified. "Obviously, if you create one type of computer offense, then another type of computer offense, you are a second time offender, and should be treated more harshly."[2]

Changing the Mind Set

While changes in the law may help those who arrest and prosecute computer criminals, changes in attitude are more likely to prevent commission of crimes in the first place, say the experts.

"One answer is educating users about computer ethics," says the FBI's Harold Hendershot. "We need more computer ethics courses in public schools, and in universities, that teach not only the use of computers, but what they mean to society as a whole. . . . When a computer is used to commit a crime, it becomes a weapon, and we need to get that message across."[3]

According to Purdue University's Eugene Spafford, users who set an example for responsible computing can help. "If the guy down the hall from me is stealing computer time in support of a business he's running on the side, I may decide that's an O.K. thing to do. Furthermore, if my manager is making illegal copies of software, because the company doesn't want to pay for it, and his boss is monitoring everybody's electronic mail to see what they are talking about, that creates an environment that says, 'The computer is a big electronic playground. Why should I be concerned?'"[4]

Why, indeed, should we be concerned? "You may not be interested in computers, but there are a lot of computers interested in you," answers Bruce Koball, general chair for CFP '93, CPSR's Third Conference on Computers, Freedom and Privacy. According to Koball, that's why everyone—from students to consumers to corporate executives—should know how computers and telecommunications can affect their lives and the society in which they live.

"These technologies hold great promise," Koball continues. "They can provide us convenience, improve our productivity and enhance our health and safety. They can also help increase public participation in government and the democratic process, and bring people together in real and virtual [electronic] communities worldwide.

"But they can also pose grave threats," he warns. "Personal privacy is increasingly at risk from invasion by the unblinking eye of computer technology. Virtually everything someone does—from buying groceries to visiting a doctor—now leaves a series of 'data points,' little electronic footprints that can be collected and tracked with increasing ease as computer systems become linked together."

As information becomes the "commodity of the future," Koball points out that control over it will become increasingly important. In fact, controlling information has already become a battleground for competing interests, such as privacy advocates and the information industry, government agencies and communications-service providers, law enforcement officials and computer hackers.[5]

As with any technological tool, we can use the gift wisely, or as a means of destruction. We can benefit from the access computers provide to global communication and information exchange. Or we can choose to exploit the electronic neighborhood for personal gain, and in the process force others to surrender personal freedoms and privacy.

Kenneth van Wyk, of Carnegie Mellon University's Computer Emergency Response Team, recently explained the choices to his ten-year-old nephew, a budding computer wizard. "I told him there is this terrific pool of electronic information out there, and you can learn a lot from it, and contribute much to it. But you still have to respect the property of others, and the rights of others. Just because you are connecting to something electronically doesn't change the basic laws of good citizenship. You still have to respect rules and regulations. If you can work within those rules and regulations, there is a wonderful world out there to explore."[6]

Cyberspace may be one of the last frontiers open to exploration. But as is true of any frontier we have tamed over the course of history, living together in harmony must eventually come first over forever roaming freely through the landscape.

Glossary

Arpanet—The world's first large computer network, named for its developer, the Pentagon's Advanced Research Projects Agency. The network became operational in 1969, linking together computers used by researchers for the U. S. Department of Defense.

Bill of Rights—The first ten amendments to the United States Constitution.

binary code—The programs that run computers are made up of a complex series of 1s and zeros, called a binary code.

binary digit—Either a 1 or a zero—represented by low-voltage and high-voltage current applied to switches (transistors) inside the microchips of a computer. Also called a bit.

bit—A binary digit, represented by a 1 or a zero.

boot infector—A type of computer virus that attaches itself to that section of a floppy or hard disk that allows the computer to "boot up," or load operating programs.

bootlegging—Making copies of commercial software for illegal resale.

bulletin board—A means of exchanging information via computer. Bulletin boards consist of a computer, special software, and a modem for taking incoming calls. The first computer bulletin board for PCs was started in 1978.

byte—A byte equals eight bits, or single binary digits, and is the basic unit of measuring memory in computing.

carders—Hackers who steal credit card numbers for re-sale, or for personal use.

central processing unit (CPU)—The computer's brain. Part of the system unit, the CPU runs the programs that tell a computer which functions to perform.

computer languages—Short letter combinations used by programmers to relay instructions to computers.

computer security—Methods used to keep unauthorized users out of a computer system.

cracker—Slang term for someone who gains unauthorized entry into a computer system.

cyberspace—A term for computer networks coined in 1982 by science fiction writer William Gibson.

data diddling—The act of changing data going into a computer, or during output from a computer, without authorization.

disk drives—Housed in a computer's system unit. The disk drive reads and writes information to or from a diskette, and may be floppy or fixed.

diskette—A floppy or removable computer disk.

dumpster diving—Sifting through a company's or an organization's trash, to get unauthorized information about a computer system.

encryption—A method of scrambling computer communication, to keep intruders from gaining information.

ethics—A branch of philosophy concerned with right and wrong, and other questions of morality.

extortion—The criminal offense of taking money or information from someone by intimidation, or through the illegal use of power, position, or knowledge.

felony—A crime punishable by at least one year in jail, or death.

fiberoptic lines—Specially designed bundles of transparent fibers, used in telecommunications to transmit telephone signals as rapid pulses of light.

First Amendment—The first article of the Bill of Rights. The First Amendment forbids Congress from tampering with the freedoms of religion, speech, assembly, and the press.

fixed disk—Also called a hard disk. The fixed disk cannot be removed from the computer, and holds much more information than a removable, or floppy diskette.

flamer—Someone who abuses computer bulletin board privileges by behaving obnoxiously or outrageously on-line.

floppy diskette—A removable disk or diskette that fits into the disk drive of a computer.

forfeiture—The right of the government, conferred by law, to take property used in committing a crime, or acquired as the result of criminal activity.

Fourteenth Amendment—An amendment to the United States Constitution that says no state may "deprive any person of life, liberty, or property without due process of law."

general executable program infector—The most dangerous type of computer virus, because it can spread to any program used by the computer.

hack value—Status given a computer user for an especially clever or knowledgeable electronic deed.

hacker—One who is an expert at operating a computer. The term has come to mean one who enters a computer system without authorization.

hardware—The physical equipment, both basic and optional, that makes up a computer system.

Internet—A complex of computer networks developed in the mid-1980s. The Internet now links nearly 900,000 computers worldwide, via telephone lines.

keyboard—A device patterned after the keys on a typewriter, which is used to type into the computer the commands and information needed to run a program.

kilobyte (K)—One K equals 1,024 bytes. A unit of measurement for computer memory.

logic bomb—Also called a time bomb. Code that tells the computer to perform a certain function at a certain time. These programs differ from a common virus, in that they do not reproduce themselves.

mainframe computers—Large computers used by big businesses and government agencies to perform large-scale tasks. They average over 10^8 operations per second.

megabyte (Mb)—One Mb equals 1,048,576 bytes. A unit of measurement for computer memory.

memory—The part of the computer that stores information to be processed by the central processing unit. Memory is of two types—ROM or "read only memory" and RAM or "random access memory"—and is measured in bytes.

microchip—See **microprocessor**.

microprocessor—Also called microchip. They are tiny wafers of silicon containing a series of electrical circuits. They relay the electrical impulses that operate the computer.

minicomputers—They have a memory capacity greater than personal computers, and are purchased by small businesses, to keep personnel and payroll records, track inventory, and perform other business functions. They process over 10^6 operations per second.

modem—Short for "modulator-demodulator," this device allows computers to communicate, over ordinary telephone lines. It converts the computer's digital pulses (a series of 1s and zeros) to analog (continuous) waves, which can be transmitted over telephone lines. A modem attached to the receiving computer translates analog signals to digital pulses, which can be read by the computer.

monitor—The televisionlike screen that displays information typed into the computer, and lets the user interact with the machine.

network—A system that allows linked computers to exchange information over telephone lines.

on-line—The term used for communicating with another computer, over telephone lines.

password—A computer security method whereby users are assigned a code word or phrase, which they must use in order to gain access to shared computer files.

personal computer (PC)—Small desktop, or personal computers are most often bought for home and school use. They perform functions at an average rate of 10^5 operations per second.

personal identification number (PIN)—The number assigned to credit card, telephone calling card, and automatic teller machine users that lets them charge services, receive cash, or otherwise access their account.

phone phreaks—A slang term for computer users who gain unauthorized entry into computer systems used by the telephone company.

piggy-backing—A method of obtaining another's personal identification number, by looking over the user's shoulder while a transaction is in progress. See also **shoulder-surfing.**

printer—A device that may be attached to a computer which will print out information on paper.

private branch-exchange (PBX)—A phone system used by businesses and other organizations that has a feature allowing employees to dial into the home office—usually on an 800 line—from outside. Using a PIN, they can then dial out again through the PBX, making long distance calls as if they were at work.

punched cards—Paper cards with holes punched in them that were once used to transmit information to computers. They became obsolete with the invention of transistors.

random access memory (RAM)—Used to temporarily store and retrieve any information coming in to the computer. If it is not first stored to disk, data stored in RAM is lost when the computer is turned off.

read only memory (ROM)—Permanently stores information that the computer needs to operate when it is turned on. Unlike RAM, the data in ROM is not lost when the computer is turned off.

salami slicing—A form of data diddling that occurs when a computer operator steals small amounts from a large number of sources, through electronic changing of data (like slicing thin pieces from a roll of salami).

shareware—Programs freely shared by computer operators who use bulletin boards or other types of electronic exchange.

shoulder-surfing—A method of stealing personal identification numbers by looking over the shoulders of legitimate customers while they are using telephone calling cards or automatic teller machines. See also **piggy-backing**

social engineering—Acquiring privileged information by using charm and technical data to convince a company insider that one is entitled to the information.

software—The term for the instructions that make a computer perform its various functions.

software piracy—Stealing information in the form of software, either for resale or for personal use.

supercomputers—Large computers used extensively by researchers and others to solve complex problems, and to map complicated data, such as the distances between stars, or the wind patterns in a storm. They average 10^{10} operations per second.

system infector—A type of computer virus which gains control after the computer is booted up. System infectors enter operating system files, such as the MS-DOS files, COPY, DIR, and ERASE.

system unit—The heart of the computer, consisting of the central processing unit (CPU), memory, disk drives, and various adapters and options.

time bomb—See **logic bomb**.

transistors—The basic device used as a fast switch in computer microchips. An electronic device that can transform weak electrical signals into strong ones. It is usually made of silicon.

trap doors—Holes written into software programs, which give programmers an easy entrance for maintenance. This hidden code can also provide unauthorized access to the savvy user, by skirting normal security procedures.

trashing—See **dumpster-diving.**

trespass—A term used for the act of gaining unauthorized or illegal access to a computer system.

Trojan horse—A destructive computer program disguised as an innocent one. Named for the fabled Greek warriors who were smuggled into Troy hidden inside a giant wooden horse.

vaccine—A program designed to locate and/or destroy a computer virus.

vacuum tubes—Glass, gas-filled cylinders used before the invention of transistors to regulate the flow of electricity inside computers. The tubes were controlled by dozens of switches that had to be set by hand.

virus—Destructive code designed to reproduce itself inside a computer and destroy or alter data.

wire fraud—A criminal act whereby the telephone system is used to steal or extort money or information.

worm—Computer code that reproduces itself like a virus, and can cause a computer to crash. A worm is not a true virus, because it does not destroy data.

Chapter Notes

Chapter 1

1. John McAfee, and Colin Haynes, *Computer Viruses, Worms, Data Diddlers, Killer Programs, and Other Threats to Your System* (New York: St. Martin's Press, 1989) p. 7.

2. Philip Elmer-De Witt, "The Kid Put Us Out of Action," *Time,* November 14, 1988, p. 76.

Chapter 2

1. Betsy Miner, "Computer 'Fatal' to Hartford, Conn., Voters," *USA Today,* September 30, 1992, p. A1.

2. Donal Kevin Gordon, Peter Pocock, and Bruce Webster, *How Things Work—Computers,* (Alexandria, Va.: Time-Life Books, 1990), p. 11.

3. Dilys Pegler Winegrad, "History and Context," *Bicentennial Celebration for ENIAC, 1986,* (Philadelphia: University of Pennsylvania Office of Public Relations, 1986).

4. *The Computerized Society,* (Alexandria, Va.: Time-Life Books, 1987), p. 24.

5. Ibid., pp. 23–24.

6. John McAfee, and Colin Haynes, *Computer Viruses, Worms, Data Diddlers, Killer Programs, and Other Threats to Your System* (New York: St. Martin's Press, 1989) p. 29.

7. *The Computerized Society,* p. 8.

8. Tracy LaQuey with Jeanne C. Ryer, *The Internet Companion—A Beginner's Guide to Global Networking,* (New York: Addison-Wesley Publishing Co., 1993), p. 7.

9. Gordon, Pocock, and Webster, pp. 124–125.

10. Electronic Frontier Foundation, "The Open Platform" (a report), (Cambridge, Mass.: Electronic Frontier Foundation: 1992), p. 4.

11. Kevin Maney, "Can Congress Pave Information Highway?" *USA Today,* January 20, 1993, p. 1B.

12. August Bequai, *Techno-Crimes: The Computerization of Crime and Terrorism,* (Lexington, Mass.: Lexington Books, 1987), p. 52.

13. Donn B. Parker, *Crime by Computer,* (New York: Charles Scribner's Sons, 1976), pp. 14, 18.

14. JJ Buck BloomBecker, ed., "Commitment to Security," (a report) (Santa Cruz, Ca.: National Center for Computer Crime Data, 1989), p. 23.

15. Peter Stephenson, "Assessing Security," *LAN Magazine,* February 1990, p. 100.

16. George Heidekat, "Happy Birthday CERT," Background material on CERT. From Software Engineering Institute, Carnegie Mellon University, Pittsburgh, Pa., December 3, 1992, p. 1.

17. John Perry Barlow, "Crime and Puzzlement: Desperados of the Datasphere" (booklet) (Cambridge Mass.: Electronic Frontier Foundation, 1990), p. 2.

Chapter 3

1. Bill Landreth, *Out of the Inner Circle—A Hacker's Guide to Computer Security,* (Bellevue, Wash.: Microsoft Press, 1985), p. 10.

2. Guy Steele, *The Hacker's Dictionary: A Guide to the World of Computer Wizards* (New York: Harper & Row, 1983), p. 79.

3. Harold Hendershot (Supervisory Special Agent, Computer Fraud and Abuse, FBI), interview with author, January 19, 1993.

4. Joan McCord, Ph.D. (Professor of Criminal Justice, Temple University), interview with author, December 8, 1992.

5. Scott Charney (Chief of the Computer Crime Unit, U.S. Department of Justice), interview with author, January 6, 1993.

6. Eugene Spafford, Ph.D. (Assistant Professor of Computer Sciences, Purdue University), interview with author, May 7, 1991.

7. Marty Flynn (Computer and Network Security Specialist, AT&T), interview with author, December 15, 1992.

8. Chris Goggans, "Hackers Aren't the Real Enemy," *Computerworld,* June 8, 1992, p. 37.

9. Tom Forester, and Perry Morrison, *Computer Ethics—Cautionary Tales and Ethical Dilemmas in Computing,* (Cambridge, Mass.: The MIT Press, 1990), p. 10.

10. Donn B. Parker, *Crime by Computer,* (New York: Charles Scribner's Sons, 1976), p. 12.

11. William S. Sessions, "Computer Crimes—An Escalating Crime Trend," *FBI Law Enforcement Bulletin,* February, 1991, pp. 12–15.

12. Mark Skandera and Marlanne Swanson, "Computer Security Bulletin Board System User's Guide," (Gaithersburg, Md.: U.S. Deptartment of Commerce, National Institute of Standards and Technology, Computer Security Division, September, 1991), p. 1.

13. Bruce Sterling, *The Hacker Crackdown—Law and Disorder on the Electronic Frontier,* (New York: Bantam Books, 1992), pp. 77, 85.

14. Richard H. Baker, *Computer Security Handbook,* (Blue Ridge Summit, Pa.: Tab Books, 1991), p. 4.

15. Jeffrey A. Hoffer, and Detmar W. Straub, Jr., "The 9 to 5 Underground: Are You Policing Computer Crimes?", *Sloan Management Review,* Summer 1989, pp. 37, 38.

Chapter 4

1. John Gorman, "Leader Gets Prison in $69 Million Theft," *Chicago Tribune,* September 21, 1989, p. 1D.

2. *Federal Reporter,* 2nd Series, (St. Paul, Minn.: West Publishing Co., 1980). 637 F.2d 941 (1980).

3. Curt Suplee and Evelyn Richards, "Computers Vulnerable, Panel Warns; Networks Susceptible to Hackers, Accidents," *Washington Post,* December 6, 1990, p. A1.

4. Philip Elmer-DeWitt, "Forgery in the Home Office," *Time,* March 26, 1990, p. 69.

5. August Bequai, *Techno-Crimes: The Computerization of Crime and Terrorism.* (Lexington, Mass.: Lexington Books, 1987), p.55.

6. JJ Buck BloomBecker, ed., "Commitment to Security," (a report) (Santa Cruz, Ca.: National Center for Computer Crime Data, 1989), p. 29.

7. Michael Matza, "Long-distance Rip-offs Rise as 'Shoulder Surfers' Spy on Phone-card Users," *Des Moines Register,* October 31, 1992, p. 2T.

8. Tom Forester and Perry Morrison, *Computer Ethics—Cautionary Tales and Ethical Dilemmas in Computing,* (Cambridge, Mass.: The MIT Press, 1990), p. 15.

9. Julie Tamaki and Michael Connelly, "Computer Skills Aid '90s Credit Card Scam," *Los Angeles Times,* August 23, 1992, p. 1B.

10. "Card Tricks—Connecticut Banks Report ATM Fraud," *Minneapolis Star & Tribune,* May 13, 1993, p. A–5.

11. *Computer Security,* (Alexandria, Va.: Time-Life Books, 1986), p. 18.

12. Bequai, p. 115.

13. Tamaki and Connelly, p. 1B.

14. Ibid.

15. Donn B. Parker, *Fighting Computer Crime*, (New York: Charles Scribner's Sons, 1983), pp. 75, 76.

Chapter 5

1. Donn B. Parker, *Fighting Computer Crime*, (New York: Charles Scribner's Sons, 1983), p. 176.

2. Ibid., pp. 170-180.

3. Bruce Sterling, *The Hacker Crackdown—Law and Disorder on the Electronic Frontier*, (New York: Bantam Books, 1992), p. vii.

4. Parker, p. 172.

5. Steve Ditlea, *Digital Deli*, (New York: Workman Publishing, 1984), p. 58.

6. Ibid., p. 60.

7. Katie Hafner and John Markoff, *Cyberpunk—Outlaws and Hackers on the Computer Frontier*, (New York: Simon & Schuster, 1991), p. 10.

8. Michael Matza, "Long-distance Rip-offs Rise as 'Shoulder Surfers' Spy on Phone-card Users," *Des Monies Register*, October 31, 1992, p. 1T.

9. Jodi Wilgoren, "Ring May be Responsible for Freeway Call Box Scam," *Los Angeles Times*, October 24, 1992, p. 4B.

10. Philip Elmer-Dewitt, "Cyberpunks and the Constitution," *Time*, April 8, 1991, p. 91.

11. Joshua Quittner, "The Charge of the Carders," *Newsday*, May 26, 1992, p. 45.

12. "Hackers Indicted," *USA Today*, July 9, 1992, p. 1B.

13. "News," *Chicago Tribune*, April 29, 1990, p. 6.

14. Shari Steele, Staff Attorney, "Classifying Hobbyist Electronic Bulletin Boards," (Cambridge, Mass.: Electronic Frontier Foundation, 1992), p. 1.

15. James Daly and Thomas Hoffman, "Wiretap Snares Alleged Hackers," *Computerworld,* July 13, 1992, p. 1.

16. Andy Zipser, "Terrible Toll," *Barron's,* November 25, 1991, p. 26.

Chapter 6

1. Dorothy E. Denning, "The United States vs. Craig Neidorf—A Debate on Electronic Publishing, Constitutional Rights and Hacking," *Communications of the ACM,* March 1991, Vol. 34, No. 3, pp. 24–43.

2. Bruce Sterling, *The Hacker Crackdown—Law and Disorder on the Electronic Frontier.* (New York: Bantam Books, 1992), pp. 102–105.

3. Tom Forester and Perry Morrison, *Computer Ethics—Cautionary Tales and Ethical Dilemmas in Computing,* (Cambridge, Mass.: The MIT Press, 1990), p. 27.

4. "Phone Access to Air Force Computers Was Child's Play," *Kansas City Star,* June 21, 1989, p. 12C.

5. Juan J. Walte, "Pentagon's Hacker 'Welcome,'" *USA Today,* September 9, 1991, p. 1A.

6. "Hot Line Can Put Software Pirates in Hot Water," *Los Angeles Times,* November 16, 1992, p. 2D.

7. Joshua Quittner, "Interview With Ice Man and Maniac...," *Newsday,* July 22, 1992, p. 83.

8. Alfred Lubrano, "Couple of Bumbling Kids," *Newsday,* April 24, 1992, p. 33.

9. Paul Mungo and Bryan Clough, *Approaching Zero—The Extraordinary Underworld of Hackers, Phreakers, Virus Writers, and Keyboard Criminals,* (New York: Random House, 1992), pp. 35, 36.

10. Robert Cross, "Computer Cops Put Byte on Fraud," *Chicago Tribune,* August 25, 1986, p. 1C.

Chapter 7

1. "Drop The Phone," *Time,* January 9, 1989, p. 49.

2. Katie Hafner and John Markoff, *Cyberpunk—Outlaws and Hackers on the Computer Frontier,* (New York: Simon & Schuster, 1991), pp. 342–344.

3. Associated Press, "Supermarket Clerks Capture Fugitive 'Dark Dante'...," *San Francisco Chronicle,* April 15, 1991, p. A16.

4. August Bequai, *Techno-Crimes: The Computerization of Crime and Terrorism.* (Lexington, Mass.: Lexington Books, 1987), pp. 34, 35.

5. *Computer Security,* (Alexandria, Va.: Time-Life Books, 1986), p. 10.

6. Tom Forester and Perry Morrison, *Computer Ethics—Cautionary Tales and Ethical Dilemmas in Computing,* (Cambridge, Mass.: The MIT Press, 1990), p. 3.

7. Katie Hafner, "Is Your Computer Secure?" *Business Week,* August 1, 1988, p. 64.

8. Joshua Quittner, "Hackers Admit Computer Crimes," *Newsday,* December 3, 1992, p. 8.

9. Bill Landreth, *Out of the Inner Circle—A Hacker's Guide to Computer Security,* (Bellevue, Wash.: Microsoft Press, 1985), pp. 35, 36.

10. Hafner and Markoff, pp. 139–250.

11. "Hackers Cracked Gulf War Data," *Newsday,* November 22, 1991, p. 17.

Chapter 8

1. D'Arcy Jenish, "A 'Terrorist' Virus," *Maclean's,* March 16, 1992, pp. 48–50.

2. Joshua Quittner, "Michelangelo Bug Could Strike Again," *Newsday,* March 6, 1992, p. 19.

3. Michael Rogers, "Not Too Much of a Headache," Newsweek, March 16, 1992, p. 60.

4. Bill Landreth, *Out of the Inner Circle—A Hacker's Guide to Computer Security,* (Bellevue, Wash.: Microsoft Press, 1985), pp. 95–97.

5. Mark Potts, "Hacker Pleads Guilty in AT&T Case," *Washington Post,* March 23, 1991, p. A1.

6. Tom Forrester and Perry Morrison, *Computer Ethics—Cautionary Tales and Ethical Dilemmas in Computing,* (Cambridge, Mass.: The MIT Press, 1990), p. 16.

7. Information Technology Association of America (press release), March 6, 1992, p. 3.

8. John Schneidawind, "Students Arrested in Spread of Mac Virus," *USA Today,* May 21, 1992, p. 7B.

Chapter 9

1. Michael Alexander, "Operation Sundevil Nabs First Suspect," *Computerworld,* February 17, 1992, p. 15.

2. Gareth Branwyn, "Computers, Crime, and the Law," *The Futurist,* September-October, 1990, p. 48.

3. Rory J. O'Connor, "Computer Hackers Seeking to Rectify Public Image," *Chicago Tribune.* December 4, 1989, p. 10N.

4. Barbara Kantrowitz with Joshua Cooper Raro, "A Woodstock for Hackers and 'Phreaks,'" *Newsweek,* August 16, 1993, pp. 47, 48.

5. Sharon Begley, "The Code of the Future," *Newsweek,* June 7, 1993, p. 70.

6. Jay Thorwaldson (Media Coordinator, CFP '93), interview with author, July 28, 1993.

7. Don Clark, "27th Amendment Proposed for High-Tech," *San Francisco Chronicle,* March 27, 1991, p. C1.

8. John Perry Barlow, "Crime and Puzzlement: Desperados of the Datasphere" (booklet), (Cambridge, Mass.: Electronic Frontier Foundation, 1990), p. 23.

9. Linda P. Campbell, "U.S. Raid Stirs Drive for Computer Rights," *Chicago Tribune,* July 11, 1990, p. 6C.

10. Chris Goggans, "Hackers Aren't the Real Enemy," *Computerworld,* June 8, 1992, p. 37.

11. James Daly and Thomas Hoffman, "Wiretap Snares Alleged Hackers," *Computerworld,* July 13, 1992, p. 1.

12. Harold Hendershot (Supervisory Special Agent, Computer Fraud and Abuse, FBI), interview with author, January 19, 1993.

13. Curt Suplee and Evelyn Richards, "Computers Vulnerable Panel Warns," *Washington Post,* December 6, 1990, p. A1.

14. Eugene Spafford, Ph.D. (Assistant Professor of Computer Sciences, Purdue University), interview with author, May 7, 1991.

15. Kenneth van Wyk (Technical Coordinator, Computer Emergency Response Team, Carnegie Mellon University), interview with author, December 2, 1992.

16. Scott Charney (Chief of the Computer Crime Unit, U.S. Department of Justice), interview with author, January 6, 1993.

17. Bill Landreth, *Out of the Inner Circle—A Hacker's Guide to Computer Security,* (Bellevue, Wash.: Microsoft Press, 1985), p. 207.

18. Harold Hendershot interview.

Chapter 10

1. Bruce Sterling, *The Hacker Crackdown—Law and Disorder on the Electronic Frontier,* (New York: Bantam Books, 1992), p. 85.

2. Scott Charney (Chief of Computer Crime Unit, U.S. Department of Justice), interview with author, January 6, 1993.

3. Harold Hendershot (Supervisory Special Agent, Computer Fraud and Abuse, FBI), interview with author, January 19, 1993.

4. Eugene Spafford, Ph.D. (Assistant Professor of Computer Sciences, Purdue University), interview with author May 7, 1991.

5. Bruce R. Koball and Jay Thorwaldson, "CFP '93" (press release), (Palo Alto, Calif.: Computer Professionals for Social Responsibility, January 11, 1993).

6. Kenneth van Wyk (Technical Coordinator, Computer Emergency Response Team, Carnegie Mellon University), interview with author, December 2, 1992.

Further Reading

Bear, John. *Computer Wimp No More.* Berkeley, Calif.: Ten Speed Press, 1992.

Bequai, August. *Techno-Crimes: The Computerization of Crime and Terrorism.* Lexington, Mass.: Lexington Books, 1987.

Forester, Tom and Perry Morrison. *Computer Ethics—Cautionary Tales and Ethical Dilemmas in Computing.* Cambridge, Mass.: The MIT Press, 1990.

Hafner, Katie and John Markoff. *Cyberpunk—Outlaws and Hackers on the Computer Frontier.* New York: Simon & Schuster, 1991.

Landreth, Bill. *Out of the Inner Circle—A Hackers Guide to Computer Security.* Bellevue, Wash.: Microsoft Press, 1985.

LaQuey, Tracy with Jeanne C. Ryer. *The Internet Companion—A Beginner's Guide to Global Networking.* New York: Addison-Wesley Publishing Co., 1993.

McAfee, John and Colin Haynes. *Computer Viruses, Worms, Data Diddlers, Killer Programs, and Other Threats to Your System.* New York: St. Martin's Press, 1989.

Mungo, Paul and Bryan Clough. *Approaching Zero—The Extraordinary Underworld of Hackers, Phreakers, Virus Writers, and Keyboard Criminals.* New York: Random House, 1992.

Steele, Guy. *The Hacker's Dictionary: A Guide to the World of Computer Wizards.* New York: Harper & Row, 1983.

Sterling, Bruce. *The Hacker Crackdown—Law and Disorder on the Electronic Frontier.* New York: Bantam Books, 1992.

Stoll, Clifford. *The Cuckoo's Egg, Tracking a Spy Through the Maze of Computer Espionage.* New York: Doubleday, 1989.

Index

revenge, 72
rival hacker groups, 73

S

salami slicing, 51, 52
Security Handbook, The,
    40, 43
shoulder-surfing, 47, *49*
social engineering, 59
software, 22
software piracy, 68
Software Publishers
    Association (SPA),
    68
Spafford, Eugene, 36,
    94, 96, 97, 104
Sterling, Bruce, 40, 54,
    101
Stoll, Clifford, 74
supercomputers, 20
system infectors, 80
system unit, 23

T

techno-bandits, 43–52
Techno-Crimes, The
    Computerization of
    Crime and
    Terrorism, 29
Thorwaldson, Jay, 90,
    91
Thunder, Susan, 72
transistors, 14
trapdoors, 82
trashing, 59
Trojan horse, 81
Twenty-seventh
    Amendment, 91

U

unauthorized access, 38
unintentional damage,
    73
updating the law, 103
U.S. Secret Service
    (USSS), 39

V

vaccine, 83
vacuum tubes, 14
van Wyk, Kenneth, 95,
    106
victims, 45–50
virus prevention, 84, 85
viruses, 6, 77–80

W

War Games, 19, 67
white-collar criminals,
    52
Wide Area Networks
    (WANs), 27
wireless
    communication, 29
wiretaps, 61
worm, 6, 81